Dig

## The Berkeley Tanner Lectures

The Tanner Lectures on Human Values were established by the American scholar, industrialist, and philanthropist Obert Clark Tanner; they are presented annually at nine universities in the United States and England. The University of California, Berkeley became a permanent host of annual Tanner Lectures in the academic year 2000–2001. This work is the seventh in a series of books based on the Berkeley Tanner Lectures. The volumes include a revised version of the lectures that Jeremy Waldron presented at Berkeley in April 2009, together with the responses of the three invited commentators on that occasion—Wai Chee Dimock, Don Herzog, and Michael Rosen—and a final rejoinder by Professor Waldron. The volumes are edited by Meir Dan-Cohen, who also contributes an introduction. The Berkeley Tanner Lecture Series was established in the belief that these distinguished lectures, together with the lively debates stimulated by their presentation in Berkeley, deserve to be made available to a wider audience. Additional volumes are in preparation.

MARTIN JAY
R. JAY WALLACE
*Series Editors*

Volumes Published in the Series

# Dignity, Rank, and Rights

JEREMY WALDRON

*With Commentaries by*
WAI CHEE DIMOCK
DON HERZOG
MICHAEL ROSEN

*Edited and Introduced by*
MEIR DAN-COHEN

# OXFORD
## UNIVERSITY PRESS

Oxford University Press is a department of the University of Oxford.
It furthers the University's objective of excellence in research, scholarship,
and education by publishing worldwide.

Oxford   New York
Auckland   Cape Town   Dar es Salaam   Hong Kong   Karachi
Kuala Lumpur   Madrid   Melbourne   Mexico City   Nairobi
New Delhi   Shanghai   Taipei   Toronto

With offices in
Argentina   Austria   Brazil   Chile   Czech Republic   France   Greece
Guatemala   Hungary   Italy   Japan   Poland   Portugal   Singapore
South Korea   Switzerland   Thailand   Turkey   Ukraine   Vietnam

Oxford is a registered trade mark of Oxford University Press
in the UK and certain other countries.

Published in the United States of America by
Oxford University Press
198 Madison Avenue, New York, NY 10016

"Dignity, Rank, and Rights" by Jeremy Waldron was delivered
as a Tanner Lecture on Human Values
at the University of California, Berkeley, April 21, 2009 and April 22, 2009.
Printed with the permission of the Tanner Lectures on Human Values, a corporation,
University of Utah, Salt Lake City.

Library of Congress Cataloging-in-Publication Data
Waldron, Jeremy.
Dignity, rank, and rights / Jeremy Waldron ; with commentaries
by Wai Chee Dimock, Don Herzog, Michael Rosen ; edited and introduced by Meir Dan-Cohen.
p. cm.
"Delivered as a Tanner lecture on human values at the University of California, Berkeley,
April 21, 2009 and April 22, 2009"—T.p. verso.
Includes bibliographical references and index.
ISBN 978-0-19-991543-9 (hardcover : alk. paper); 978-0-19-023544-4 (paperback : alk. paper)
1. Philosophical anthropology.   2. Dignity.   3. Civil rights.
4. Human rights.   I. Dan-Cohen, Meir.   II. Title.
BD450.W233 2012
128'.3—dc23        2012000941

# Contents

## REPLY TO COMMENTATORS

# Contributors

JEREMY WALDRON is Chichele Professor of Social and Political Theory at All Souls College, Oxford, a chair he holds jointly with his position as University Professor at New York University Law School. Professor Waldron's work in jurisprudence and political theory is well known, as are his articles on constitutionalism, democracy, homelessness, judicial review, minority cultural rights, property, rule of law, and torture. His books include *The Dignity of Legislation* (Cambridge University Press, 1999), *Law and Disagreement* (Oxford University Press, 1999), *Torture, Terror and Trade-offs: Philosophy for the White House* (Oxford University Press, 2010), and *The Harm in Hate Speech* (Harvard University Press, 2012). Professor Waldron was elected to the American Academy of Arts and Sciences in 1998, the British Academy in 2011, and in 2011 he also received the Phillips Prize from the American Philosophical Society for lifetime achievement in jurisprudence.

MEIR DAN-COHEN is Milo Reese Robbins Chair in Legal Ethics, School of Law, the University of California at Berkeley and an Affiliate of the Department of Philosophy there. He works in legal and moral philosophy, with a special interest in conceptions of self and criminal law theory. His publications include *Harmful Thoughts: Essays on Law, Self, and Morality* (Princeton University Press, 2002) and *Rights, Persons, and Organizations: A Legal Theory for Bureaucratic Society* (University of California Press, 1986).

WAI CHEE DIMOCK is William Lampson Professor of English and American Studies at Yale University. Her publications include *Empire for Liberty: Melville and the Poetics of Individualism* (Princeton University Press, 1989); *Rethinking Class* (Columbia University Press, 1994); *Residues of Justice: Literature, Law, Philosophy* (University of California Press, 1995); *Through Other Continents: American Literature Across Deep Time* (Princeton University Press, 2006), and *Shades of the Planet: American Literature as World Literature* (Princeton University Press, 2007). She is now at work on a critical work: *Low Theory: Genres, Media, Webs*; and a print-and-web anthology, *American Literature in the World*.

DON HERZOG is Edson R. Sunderland Professor of Law at the University of Michigan. His main teaching interests are political, moral, legal, and social theory; constitutional interpretation; torts; and the First Amendment. His books include *Poisoning the Minds of the Lower Orders* (Princeton University Press, 1998), *Cunning* (Princeton University Press, 2006), and *Household Politics: Conflict in Early Modern England* (free online version by M-Publishing, 2012, and Yale University Press, 2013).

MICHAEL ROSEN is Professor of Government at Harvard University and Honorary Professor of Philosophy at the Humboldt University, Berlin. He works mainly on political theory and the history of philosophy. His works include *Hegel's Dialectic and its Criticism* (Cambridge University Press, 1982), *On Voluntary Servitude: False Consciousness and the Theory of Ideology* (Harvard University Press, 1996), and *Dignity: Its History and Meaning* (Harvard University Press, 2012), as well as articles and edited volumes.

# Dignity, Rank, and Rights

# Introduction: Dignity and Its (Dis)content

MEIR DAN-COHEN

In his Tanner Lectures, Professor Jeremy Waldron contributes to a rapidly growing literature on human dignity and its political and legal ramifications. Following the lectures are commentaries by Professors Michael Rosen, Don Herzog, and Wai Chee Dimock, as well as Waldron's reply. All these are engrossing, rich, generous, elegant, and short. No need for me to spoil the fun by summarily anticipating what is already accessibly before you. A better service to the readers, especially to those who have not hitherto spent much time contemplating dignity, is to provide instead some context for the lectures and the subsequent exchange. The aim is to paint a contrasting backdrop that will help appreciate the distinctive nature of Waldron's position, and indeed its audacity.

Even the most casual web-search will confirm that the term *dignity* has acquired great prominence in recent years, both in public discourse and in the philosophical literature. And where there is prominence there is often also notoriety. Dignity has many ardent devotees as well as some vocal detractors. But though all sides use the same term, it is less clear that they always address the same topic or have in mind the same concept. Dignity has come to mean different things to different people. It will be easier to provide a bird's-eye view of the terrain, and locate Waldron's position in it, if we provisionally diversify our terminology, and use not just the term *dignity*, but also two other quasi-cognates, *honor* and *worth*. Some use dignity as a synonym for or an extension of honor, whereas others consider dignity as equivalent to worth. The two terms, honor and worth, are not quite symmetrical, though. Honor is an ordinary term, and its philosophical use is for the most part in keeping with its common usage. Worth is a more specialized term, deriving its meaning in the present context primarily from Kant's moral theory. This difference in provenance of the two terms signals a more substantive difference in the conception of dignity they each designate. By employing honor and worth as two contrasting poles we can distinguish a range of senses with which *dignity* is used.

Honor and worth can be fruitfully contrasted along four dimensions: origin, scope, distribution, and grip. Honor is of social origin: it derives from and reflects one's social position and the norms and attitudes that define it; whereas worth, at least as used by Kant, has metaphysical origins: the alleged radical autonomy of the noumenal self. Consequently, honor is in principle limited in scope, capable of privileging only those who occupy certain positions while excluding others who occupy different ones; whereas worth has a universal scope, applying to every human being as such. Relatedly, the distribution of honor is typically uneven and hierarchical, reflecting and indeed in part constituting social stratification; worth is evenly distributed over humanity as a whole. Finally, the grip that worth has on its possessors (or, conversely, the grip they have on it) is much stronger than the grip of honor. Honor is contingent, in the sense that it must be earned or granted, and so can be forfeited or withdrawn; whereas worth is categorical, attaching to all its possessors by virtue of their being human, no matter what. These contrasting clusters of attributes go hand in hand with a familiar claim, to the effect that the ascendance of dignity-talk marks a trajectory from honor to worth. Since Kant, and with increasing momentum in the last few decades or so, honor has been superseded by worth as the favored interpretation of dignity.

In these lectures, Waldron swims against the current. He introduces a conception of dignity as universalized high social rank, which amounts to a reversal of this trend by tying dignity back to honor rather than to worth. To be sure, his dignity-as-rank is not the same as honor itself. Waldron most emphatically does not advocate a return to a hierarchical social system of valuation in which people's dignity varies with their social status, let alone to a state of affairs in which the dignity of some is built on the degradation of others. His conception of dignity is every bit as universal in scope and as egalitarian in distribution as that of the most devout Kantian. Waldron wholeheartedly endorses the universalization and equalization of dignity in the modern age. The question he raises and the challenge he poses concern only which notion, honor or worth, offers a sounder interpretive framework for these achievements. Since there is general agreement that the scope of dignity ought to be universal and its distribution egalitarian, the focus is on the two other dimensions of comparison, origin and grip. Waldron's preference for tying dignity to the tradition of honor rather than to the philosophy of worth is first and foremost a view that universal and equal dignity is better anchored in evolving social practice than in Kantian metaphysics.

This view is linked to another central theme in these lectures: privileging law over morality as the primary habitat and dominant source of dignity. Though the alignment need not be perfect, we generally tend to view law as a social phenomenon. Tracking dignity to its legal provenance is an astute step that leaves open difficult conundrums of moral philosophy, while allowing us to make progress on the central issues and main practical ramifications associated with the concept of dignity today.

The appeal of a social conception of dignity over a metaphysical conception is understandable, particularly when we recall that Kant's own moral theory is grounded in a metaphysics that few contemporary normative Kantians espouse. It is the metaphysics of the thing-in-itself and, relatedly, of the noumenal self, whose freedom is a matter of wholesale exemption from laws of nature, which for this purpose comprise not just physics but what we ordinarily think of as psychology as well. Moreover, as Waldron demonstrates, by leveling up and expanding a notion of honor, dignity-as-rank is capable of underwriting an equal dignity for all.

But all this comes at a price in the dimension of grip. As conceived by Waldron, the social origins of dignity cannot offer the grip that the Kantian position does. Expanding the scope of dignity and leveling it up are doubtlessly great social and legal achievements, but this is also their vulnerability. What is socially and legally granted can be socially and legally withdrawn. The worry is not about the fragility of dignity-as-rank in the face of changing winds of politics or brute force. Nothing is sturdy enough to withstand these kinds of adversities. The fragility in question is an argumentative one; it takes place in the space of reasons and justifications, not in the space of struggle and mayhem. It is here that a difference exists between, on the one hand, celebrating and cheering on the morphing of local and hierarchical honor into universal equal dignity, and, on the other hand, providing an *argument* in favor of this development that would give it some normative grounding. The challenge Waldron poses is accordingly quite formidable: can we retain the social origins of dignity while securing its categorical grip? Although this is not the place to try to meet this challenge, let me point in one general direction in which it might be met. It involves, somewhat surprisingly perhaps, not muting but amplifying the social factor Waldron highlights.

In moving in this direction we can be guided by another beacon of dignity-as-worth mentioned by Waldron: Giovanni Pico della Mirandola and his famous fifteenth-century *Oration on the Dignity of Man*.[1] Anticipating such modern strands of thought as existentialism, communitarianism, and postmodernism, Pico proclaims the theme of human self-creation: what distinguishes humanity from the rest of creation and indeed gives it its special, elevated worth is that Man has no essence, and so must create his own. Put in a more contemporary idiom, on this *constructive view* the self is the largely unintended by-product of individual actions and collective practices, whose primary orientation is not the creation of a self but the accomplishment of some individual or collective goals. By pursuing this broad theme, we move beyond the social origins of people's status or value that Waldron explores, and consider the social origins of people themselves. If the bearer of dignity is not a noumenal self, ensconced in an ethereal Kingdom of Ends located in a nether region of things-in-themselves, but a socially constructed self, the distance between dignity-as-rank and dignity-as-worth shrinks, and the two conceptions might even converge. A socially grounded conception of dignity might yet be universal, equal, and secured by categorical grip. How?

We can start from the end, the categorical grip. The problem we noted with a socially based conception of dignity is its apparent contingency: society may fail to confer equal dignity on all. This possibility does not arise under the constructive view. If the source of dignity is in human self-creation, the process by which dignity is conferred is the very same one by which the human person is constituted, and so there can be no slippage between the two. Since self-creation is an attribute of humanity, dignity associated with self-creation is also universal in scope: it is coextensive with humanity as a whole. Finally, dignity acquired through self-creation is equal, since it accrues to us qua subjects of construction rather than as its products, and so irrespective of the content and variability of what is being produced.

But why is self-creation a source of elevated worth? In one form or another, different answers have been proffered to this daunting question. The gist of the matter can be, however, briefly indicated by giving Pico's view a Kantian gloss. We can link the notion of self-creation to Kant's insistence on human intelligibility, while side-stepping the metaphysics of the noumenal self. The key is that to contend that humanity creates itself is not to maintain that we create our own organisms. Rather, human self-creation takes place in the medium of meaning: the meanings we create, create us. What in turn makes human action intelligible, what gives it meaning, is that it is done for the sake of something or other. To act intelligibly requires that that for the sake of which one acts, the end, be deemed worth pursuing, and so valuable. In this sense all human action consists in the projection and attempted realization of purported values. Since we deem these values worth pursuing, we must endorse them. This is the sense in which, in pursuing any value at all, we must recognize ourselves as the ultimate authority. To recognize ourselves as having a definitive authority over ourselves, is to defer to ourselves. This amounts to recognizing our superior worth.

As I said, more than one road leads to this conclusion, though probably none that is completely clear of potholes and bumps. Even so, human self-creation is suggestive enough, and in its various forms sufficiently imbricated in the discourse of dignity, to offer a promising supplement to Waldron's social approach. If some such connection between self-creation and human worth be granted, however, other obstacles loom large. Two in particular must be mentioned since they bear directly on Waldron's main theme. The first is a worry that appeal to human self-creation begs the crucial question as to who exactly is included in this venture: who counts as a human being for the purpose at hand? Indeed, Waldron recounts some chilling reminders of how odious our record is in this regard. But following in Pico's footsteps may in fact allay these concerns. Pico's *Oration* is a spin on the story of creation, and so he treats of humanity as one biological species among others. The thesis of human self-creation is accordingly grounded in a system of classification in which the extension of *Homo sapiens* is as naturally fixed as is the extension of *Loxodonta africana*. *Who* is a human being is a given; *what* she is, is not.

To be sure, the capacity for self-creation requires that the conception of humanity as a biological species be overlaid with another order of signification in which the organism is endowed with meaning and so made intelligible. But attending to the meanings that distinguish *humanity* from other species does not undo the biological extension of the term. Think by analogy of the relationship in the case of books between the physical volume and, say, the novel it contains. Irrelevant complications aside, the extension of *book* in some library would be the same irrespective of whether one were to attend to the volumes or to the novels. For example, one can confidently count the books even if, unable to read, one could not tell apart *Anna Karenina* from *The Old Man and the Sea*.

This reassurance that the contours of dignity encompass the entire human race leaves open, however, a second cardinal question about the subject of self-creation pertinent to the social orientation of Waldron's lectures. Human self-creation can be given a collective interpretation, as involving humanity as a whole, or a distributive interpretation, according to which each individual forges her own identity. *The social construction of the self*, which fixes on society as the arena of human self-creation, is intermediate between these poles. Now since Waldron dwells particularly on the social (and relatedly legal) origins of dignity, to bring the self-creation theme into alignment with his approach would seem to require that we adopt this third interpretation.

The choice between the universal, the social, and the individual as the site of self-creation does not appear to be easy, however, and so it may come as some relief that no such choice is necessary, or indeed possible, since each of the interpretations implies the others as well. To see the point, reconsider the picture of the social as intermediate between the individual and the universal. Intermediate in what dimension? One answer would be numerical, as *many* is intermediate between *one* and *all*. But the view of self-creation as manifesting human intelligibility and as occurring in the medium of meaning suggests another answer. Meanings are abstract, and so the difference can be conceived as a matter of levels of abstraction: the social is more abstract than the individual, and the universal, yet more abstract. Or stated in reverse, social meanings are a more concrete elaboration of universal meaning, and individual meanings a further and yet more concrete elaboration of social ones.

This dovetails with the earlier observation that self-creation comes in the form of pursuing ends and so endorsing values. The particular ends that I espouse and the values that I so endorse define the distinctive content of my life and distinguish it from that of others. But if to encounter a human being is to encounter an intelligible being, it is to encounter a being with whom communication and hence mutual interpretation and understanding are in principle possible. For this to be the case, I must be able to see another's values, no matter how different from mine, as *values*, that is as ends capable of making sense of her life in the same way that my values make of mine. And so, in fixing my own identity, I must view myself as enacting and articulating a more abstract identity: my identity as a human being, which I share with everyone else. Seen in these terms, *humanity* labels at a high level of abstraction the meaning that every human being expresses or enacts in endlessly ramified and divergent ways. Within the same picture, the *social* designates a concatenation of meanings at an intermediate level of abstraction, between the individual and the universal. Focusing on it and privileging it, the way Waldron does, does not threaten to displace the universal or the individual standpoints. It only amounts to the view that the social is a particularly fecund source of meanings, and so is especially vital to the process of human self-creation and its study.

But enough with preliminaries; time now for the main treat.

## Note

1. Giovanni Pico della Mirandola, *Oration on the Dignity of Man*, trans. A. Robert Caponigri (Washington, DC: Regnery Gateway 1956).

# Dignity, Rank, and Rights

JEREMY WALDRON

# Lecture 1: Dignity and Rank

## 1. Law and Morality

My subject is human dignity. Dignity, we will see, is a principle of morality and a principle of law. It is certainly a principle of the highest importance, and it ought to be something we can give a good philosophic account of. That is what I am going to try to do in these lectures.

It is a topic that we can come to through law—analyzing the preambles of various declarations of human rights, for example, or interpreting the legal rules that prohibit inhuman and degrading treatment—or it is something we can treat as, in the first instance, a moral idea.

On the second approach, which seems like a natural one to adopt, we begin with dignity as a moral idea and then we look to see how adequately or how clumsily that moral idea has been represented in the work of the drafters of statutes, constitutions, and human rights conventions or in the decisions that constitute our legal doctrines and precedents. So on this approach, before we get anywhere near the law, we look for the sense that moral philosophers have made of the concept of dignity—Immanuel Kant, for example, or modern philosophers like Stephen Darwall or James Griffin.[1]

That is a tempting approach. But moral philosophy is not our only philosophical resource for exploring an idea like dignity. What if we were to approach things from the opposite direction? Dignity seems at home in law: law is its natural habitat. We find it in many legal documents and proclamations: in the opening provision of

Germany's Basic Law, for example, in the South African constitution, and in the International Covenant on Civil and Political Rights
(ICCPR).[2] We tell ourselves that this must be a case of the law using
a moral ideal. But maybe morality has more to learn from law than
vice versa. So let us begin by analyzing how the concept works in
its legal habitat and see whether the jurisprudence of dignity can
cast any light on its use in moral discourse. Joseph Raz said to me a
few weeks before I delivered these lectures that "dignity" is not a
term that crops up much in ordinary moral conversation. Its presence is an artifact of philosophers' trying to make sense of ordinary
moral ideas (like value and respect). Like "utility," it is a constructive idea with a foundational and explicative function. If it has
been imported from law to perform this constructive function, then
we had better turn first to jurisprudence to find out something
about the distinctive *legal* ideas that the moral philosophers have
appropriated.[3]

So, for example: the moral philosophers tell us that dignity is a
matter of status. But status is a legal conception and not a simple
one.[4] Dignity, we are told, was once tied up with rank: the dignity of
a king was not the same as the dignity of bishop and neither of
them was the same as the dignity of a professor. If our modern
conception of human dignity retains any scintilla of its ancient and
historical connection with rank—and I think it does: I think it
expresses the idea of the high and equal rank of every human
person[5]—then we should look first at the bodies of law that relate
status to rank (and to right and privilege) and see what if anything
is retained of these ancient conceptions when dignity is put to work
in a new and egalitarian environment.

Dignity is intimately connected with the idea of rights—as the
ground of rights, the content of certain rights, and perhaps even the
form and structure of rights. It would be a brave moral philosopher
who would say that the best way to understand rights (or a concept
connected with rights) is to begin with moral ideas and then see
what the law does with those. Surely it is better to begin (as Hohfeld

did)[6] with rights as a juridical idea and then look to see how that works in a normative environment (like morality) that is structured quite differently from the way in which a legal system is structured.[7] I think the same may be true of dignity. Even as the ground of rights—as when we are told in the preamble to the ICCPR that the rights contained in the covenant "derive from the inherent dignity of the human person"—dignity need not be treated in the first instance as a moral idea. After all it is not just surface-level rules that are legal in character (as though anything deeper must be "moral"). I follow Ronald Dworkin in believing that grounding doctrines can be legal too—legal principles, for example, or legal policies.[8] Law creates, contains, envelops, and constitutes these ideas. It does not just borrow them from morality.

So this is the point I want to begin with: it is probably not a good idea to treat dignity as a moral conception in the first instance or assume that a philosophical explication of dignity must begin as moral philosophy. Equally we should not assume that a legal analysis of dignity is just a list of texts and precedents, in national and international law, in which the word "dignity" appears. There is such a thing as legal philosophy, there are such things as legal principles, and it is a jurisprudence of dignity, not a hornbook analysis that I will be pursuing in these lectures.

## 2. A Variety of Uses

There does not seem to be any canonical definition of "dignity" in the law. One esteemed jurist has observed that its intrinsic meaning appears to have been left to intuitive understanding.[9]

If you glance quickly at the way in which "dignity" figures in the law, you will probably get the impression that its usage is seriously confused. Dignity is defined one way in a legal document, then defined another way in a different document. As a concept it performs one sort of legal function; then the law has it performing quite a different function, locating it as a concept in a different category from the first. Moral philosophers tend to notice these things, and I am sorry to say that the indignant recording of such impressions is what passes for philosophical analysis in some circles.

In fact I think patience and thoughtfulness actually pay off in this area, as they often do in responding to destructive analytic critique. Sometimes the various ideas associated with what we suspect is an ambiguous term in fact turn out to make complementary rather than rival contributions to its meaning. Consider an analogy. Some people say that "democracy" means "rule by the people." Some say it means "political equality." Some say, with Joseph Schumpeter, that democracy is just a political system to secure stability by providing for regular competition for power among elites on an institutionalized basis.[10] Now we can see these three meanings as rival definitions if we like, and complain about the inherent confusion of the term. But we should first check whether the alleged ambiguities might not be combinable as complementary contributions to a single multifaceted idea: democracy is a system of regularized competition among political elites, organized on the basis of political equality, with the effect of giving the common people substantial control over their government. We combine the three meanings in a single consistent but complicated definition. So it might be with human dignity: we might be able to turn the tables on the destructive analytic critic, by insisting that what he reads, superficially, as ambiguity is in fact a reflection of the rich and complementary aspects of the meaning of this multifaceted term.[11]

But some of the apparent difficulties might be harder to parse. The human rights charters tell us that dignity is inherent in the human person; they also command us to make heroic efforts to establish everyone's dignity. Is this an equivocation?[12] Jeremy Bentham used to make fun of a similar dualism in the use of the term "liberty." Defenders of natural rights would say that men are born free, but would then go on to complain in the name of rights that so many of them were born into slavery.[13] "Men ought to be free because they are free, even though they are not"—was that the claim? Such reasoning, which Bentham called "absurd and miserable nonsense," seemed to veer between the incoherent and the tautological.[14] In fact the appearance of equivocation is easily dispelled. In a slave society, a person might be identified as a free man in a juridical sense—that is his legal status—even though he is found in conditions of slavery. (He may have been enslaved by mistake or kept erroneously in chains after his emancipation.) So, similarly, one might say that every human person is free as a matter of status— the status accorded to him by his creator—even though it is the case that some humans are actually in chains and need to have their freedom represented as the content of a normative demand. The premise may be problematic for those who reject its implicit metaphysics, but the overall claim is not incoherent. And the same logic may work for "dignity." On the one hand, the term may be used to convey something about the inherent rank or status of human beings; on the other hand, it may be used concomitantly to convey the demand that that rank or status should actually be respected.

A more interesting duality of uses has to do with the distinction between dignity as the ground of rights and dignity as the content of rights. On the one hand, we are told that human rights "derive from the inherent dignity of the human person." On the other hand, it is said that people have a right to be protected against "degrading treatment" and "outrages on personal dignity."[15] Dignity is what some of our rights are rights *to*; but dignity is also what grounds all of our rights. I have my doubts about the claim that rights derive from any single foundation, be it dignity, equality, autonomy, or (as it is now sometimes said) security. In any case, I want to leave this duality of ground and content in place. It is perfectly possible that human dignity could be the overall telos of rights in general, but also that certain particular rights could be oriented specifically to the explicit pursuit of that objective or to protecting it against some standard threats to dignity, while others are related to this goal in a more indirect sort of way.

I am actually going to argue against a reading of the dignity idea that makes it the goal or telos of human rights. I think it makes better sense to say that dignity is a normative status and that many human rights may be understood as incidents of that status. (The relation between a status and its incidents is not the same as the relation between a goal and the various subordinate principles that promote the goal; it is more like the relation between a set and its members.) Still, if human dignity is regarded as a rank or status, there remains a duality between general norms establishing that status and particular norms like those that prohibit degradation, which are indispensable to the support of dignity.

Here is an analogy. The relation between these two sorts of norms might be like the relation between the general status or dignity of a judge and the specific offense of contempt of court. Protection against contempt is not all that there is to being a judge, but a ban on contempt might still be thought indispensable to judicial dignity. And not just a ban on contempt; more affirmative provisions may also be important. The Constitution of Poland stipulates that "[j]udges shall be granted…remuneration consistent with the dignity of their office."[16] And there may be other accoutrements too—gowns, wigs, formal modes of address, an order of precedence at banquets. These are all important for judicial dignity. But they do not exhaust the status of a judge; her status has to do also with her role and with her powers and responsibilities.

Something analogous may be true for human dignity in general: we can distinguish between dignity as a general status and the particular rules that protect and support it. Some of these particular rules are affirmative, like the provision in the Universal Declaration of Human Rights which says that "[e]veryone who works has the right to just and favourable remuneration ensuring for himself and his family an existence worthy of human dignity."[17] And some are negative, like the ban on degrading treatment. Both kinds of protection are important. But they are not all there is to human dignity. We need to get at what dignity—the status—in general involves.

Some may see this as too ambitious. A more modest approach might simply take the various specific prohibitions on degradation at face value without necessarily assuming that they are ancillary to the broader enterprise of upholding a general rank or status of human dignity.[18] Consider the prohibitions on "degrading treatment" in the human rights covenants.[19] Should we not just say that these are intended to protect people against a very specific evil of gross humiliation, particularly in situations like detention, incarceration, hospitalization, and military captivity—situations of more or less comprehensive vulnerability with total control by others of a person's living situation? Should we not just say that that is all that these provisions are for? Why do we have to work up a general account of dignity? Surely all we require is a retail theory, which may be no more extensive than is needed to make sense of these particular prohibitions.

But even if we were to take that tack, it would still leave the question of what the law is doing when it also talks in more general (wholesale) terms about the dignity of the human person. And it does. Since we have to give an account of that *anyway*, it is surely worth striving to produce a theory that unifies what we say about dignity in general and what we say about these specific (or retail) dignitarian requirements.

## 3. Is There a Need for a Moral Foundation?

Human rights law suggests that dignity is the ground of rights: in the words of the ICCPR Preamble, rights "derive from the inherent dignity of the human person." Does this assume a moral ideal of dignity that serves as an extralegal grounding for human rights?

Not necessarily. The Covenant gives us the *legal ground* of the rights set out in the body of its text, but it is a further question whether this is supposed to be the legal representation of a moral conception. Maybe every legal idea has a moral underpinning of some sort; but it would be a mistake to think that the moral underpinning has to have the same shape or content as the legal ground.

Consider as an analogy Hannah Arendt's account of the ancient Athenian commitment to political equality among free-born male citizens. The Athenians adopted a legal principle of treating one another as equals, not because of any moral conviction about real equality between them, but because such a principle made possible a form of political community they could not otherwise have. For their engagement in the joint enterprise of politics, the community created for each of them an artificial *persona*—the citizen—that could take its place on the public stage, presenting them as equals for political purposes. The community did this using artificial techniques like the equal right to speak in the assembly, the equality of votes, the equal liability to be drafted into a jury, and so on.[20] Human dignity might be something similar. There might be a point to its legal recognition, but that point need not be an underlying moral dignity.

That is a possibility. Of course many philosophers do believe in an underlying moral dignity. In his recent book *On Human Rights*, James Griffin has defended a moral account of dignity, which he thinks underlies human rights. He adopts his conception of dignity from a fifteenth-century writer, Pico della Mirandola—though he drops most of the very substantial theology that Pico associates with dignity—and he comes to the conclusion that the key to dignity is the human capacity to "be that which he wills" (which Griffin relabels normative agency).[21] "The sort of dignity relevant to human rights," Griffin says, "is that of a highly prized status: that we are normative agents."[22] He says that our human rights are derived from our dignity, understood in this way. Sometimes the way he says this indicates that normative agency is the telos of our rights: human rights are a means to normative agency as an end; we have a right to welfare, for example, because you can't exercise normative agency when you are hungry.[23] Other times, what he says conveys the point that protecting our rights *vindicates* our normative agency (e.g., by respecting our choices), which is a rather different idea.[24]

The second of these formulations is more closely connected to dignity as status. In general a status is not a goal or a telos: a status *comprises* a given set of rights rather than defining them as instrumentalities. I am attracted to the status account, and much of the rest of these lectures is devoted to it. I mention the uncertainty in Griffin's account just so that we do not have too simple a picture of dignity as a foundation. A status account will present dignity (however defined) as foundation-*ish* (or, as we might say, foundation*al*) but it may not be a foundation in the simple way that (for example) the major value-premises of a consequential argument are a foundation of everything else in the consequentialist's moral theory.

## 4. Dignity and Bearing

We place a high value on human dignity, but height can be understood in different ways. We might just mean that dignity counts for more than other values. Or height might mean something like rank. Consider again the idea of status. Some legal statuses are low and servile, like slavery and villeinage (or, in the modern world, felony or bankruptcy). Others are quite "high," like royalty or nobility. "Highness," here, is not like moral weight (as in the moral weight of a particularly prolonged or intense episode of pleasure for the purposes of Jeremy Bentham's felicific calculus). It is more a matter of rank, and it conveys things like authority and deference.

The high character of dignity also has physical connotations—a sort of "moral orthopedics of human dignity"—what some Marxists, following Ernst Bloch, used to call "walking upright."[25] Dignity has resonances of something like noble bearing. In one of the meanings the *Oxford English Dictionary* ascribes to the term, it connotes "befitting elevation of aspect, manner, or style;…stateliness, gravity." When we hear the claim that someone has dignity, what comes to mind are ideas such as: having a certain sort of presence; uprightness of bearing; self-possession and self-control; self-presentation as someone to be reckoned with; not being abject, pitiable, distressed, or overly submissive in circumstances of adversity.[26]

These connotations resonate with what I called earlier the retail use of "dignity" in humanitarian law and human rights covenants. The ban on degrading treatment can be read as requiring that people must be permitted to present themselves (even in detention, even in the power of the police) with a modicum of self-control and self-possession.[27] I think it is a good thing in a philosophic account of dignity, not just to unite the retail and the wholesale uses of "dignity" in the law, but to do so in a way that makes illuminating sense of these intuitions about moral orthopedics. A good account of human dignity will explain it as a very general status. But it will also generate an account of it as noble bearing and an account of the importance of the ban on humiliating and degrading treatment. That is what I am trying to do with an account of dignity as a high-ranking status, comparable to a rank of nobility—only a rank assigned now to every human person, equally without discrimination: dignity as nobility for the common man.

## 5. Stipulative Uses of "Dignity"

Some philosophers' definitions of "dignity" seem quite unrelated to these themes of nobility, bearing, and nondegradation. Consider, for example, Ronald Dworkin's use of "dignity" in his book *Is Democracy Possible Here?* At the beginning of that work, Dworkin states two principles that he says "identify…abstract value in the human situation."[28] One has to do with the objective value of a human life. The other states that each person has a special responsibility for how his or her own life goes. Dworkin says: "These two principles…together define the basis and conditions of human dignity, and I shall therefore refer to them as principles or dimensions of dignity."[29] He says, quite rightly, that these principles reflect values that are deeply embedded in Western political theory. They have not always been labeled "principles of dignity," but of course there is no objection to calling them that, if this is what Dworkin wants to do. However, he nowhere suggests that the "dignity" label adds any illumination to the principles, and his elaboration of them is conducted in a way that does not rely on any specific connotations of the concept that we have noticed so far.[30]

We might just make the term mean what Dworkin says it means, by linguistic stipulation. But there is no particular reason why we should assign "dignity" to this task. Other words would do as well. We could use the word "glory," and talk about the inherent glory of the human being, respect for glory, humans having an inalienable right to glory, and so on. We would acknowledge of course that "glory" has some other connotations, which may or may not resonate with its use here, but we would say we were giving it new work to do, where it will stand for these two Dworkinian principles. I hope I will not be misunderstood as making fun of Dworkin's stipulation when I remind you that the word "glory" has a history of being used in his way.[31] It can be put to work in political philosophy just as Humpty Dumpty puts it to work in logic (as a term for a certain sort of argument). But we would have to pay it extra and it may turn out that "dignity" comes cheaper for this task, being more manageable and less temperamental.

## 6. Kant

Dworkin is in good company, for the account that I am going to give is also at odds with one of the best-known philosophical theories: the definition of dignity in Immanuel Kant's *Groundwork of the Metaphysics of Morals*:

In the kingdom of ends everything has either a price or a dignity. What has a price can be replaced by something else as its equivalent; what, on the other hand, is raised above all price and therefore admits of no equivalent has a dignity. Now, morality is the condition under which alone a rational being can be an end in itself....Hence morality, and humanity insofar as it is capable of morality, is that which alone has dignity.[32]

The first thing to say about this definition is that "dignity" here is the English translator's term, not Kant's. Kant uses the German term *Würde*. There is a well-established practice of translating *Würde* as "dignity." But the two words have slightly different connotations.[33] *Würde* is much closer to "worth" than our term "dignity" is.

The second thing to say is that although *value beyond price* and *the intrinsic nonnegotiable nonfungible worth that inheres in every human being in virtue of his or her moral capacity* are wonderful and important ideas, there is no particular reason to use our term "dignity" to convey them. *Würde*, in sense of the passage in Kant's *Groundwork*, expresses a type of value or a fact about value. "Dignity," by contrast, conveys the idea of a type of status that a person may have. The distinction may seem a fine one, particularly if we acknowledge that in moral theory a person's status can derive from an estimation of that person's fundamental worth.[34] A person may have dignity (in the sense that interests us) because he or she has worth (or *Würde* in Kant's sense): but this is genuine derivation, not synonymy. We can distinguish the ideas also in terms of appropriate responses to value and status, respectively.[35] The thing to do with something of value is promote it or protect it, perhaps maximize things of that kind, at any rate to treasure it. The thing to do with a ranking status is to respect and defer to the person who bears it. It is important not to elide this difference.

Now Kant does also say that the basis of human worth commands respect. But this is not exactly respect for persons.[36] What commands respect on Kant's account is the capacity for morality; and I agree with Michael Rosen that this is a sort of Platonism;[37] it involves respecting something within a person, not a person himself or herself. Our respect for the workings of the moral law within ourselves is subjectively a sort of quivering awe at the way the moral law can strike down our inclinations.[38] Rosen argues that it is a quasi-aesthetic ideal, and I am inclined to agree with him.

I am sure there are some readers who will regard my turning my back on the conception of dignity in the *Groundwork* as a reductio ad absurdum of my whole enterprise. "If not Kant, then who?"—they will ask. But Kant's use of dignity (or *Würde*) is complicated. He does also use the term in ways that line up much more closely to the traditional connotations of nobility that we have been talking about. In his political philosophy, Kant talks of "the distribution of dignities." He describes nobility as a dignity that "makes its possessors members of a higher estate even without any special services on their part." And he says that "no human being can be without any dignity, since he at least has the dignity of a citizen."[39] These sayings associate dignity with rank in more or less exactly the way that I want to associate them.

Additionally, *The Metaphysics of Morals* contains a long, priggish passage "On Servility," where Kant talks of our "duty with reference to the dignity of humanity within us":

Be no man's lackey.—Do not let others tread with impunity on your rights.—Contract no debt for which you cannot give full security.—Do not accept favors you could do without....Complaining and whining, even crying out in bodily pain, is unworthy of you, especially if you are aware of having deserved it....Kneeling down or prostrating oneself on the ground, even to show your veneration for heavenly objects, is contrary to the dignity of humanity....Bowing and scraping before a human being seems in any case unworthy of a human being.[40]

This Polonius-like account of dignified bearing sounds like the sort of thing I am pursuing. But the challenge is to connect all this back to what dignity is said in the *Groundwork* to be: namely, value beyond price. That is what I have trouble with. There is no doubt that Kant has some such connection in mind. The "absolute inner worth" of our moral personality begins as a basis of self-esteem, but it is also a sort of asset by which a person "exacts respect for himself from all other rational beings in the world" and measures himself "on a footing of equality with them."[41] Stephen Darwall makes much of this passage in a recent book.[42] He believes that there is an important conception of dignity to be found in Kant's work that has much more to do with the way we elicit respect for ourselves from others by making what he calls "second-person" demands on them, than with any notion of the objective preciousness of our moral capacity. Darwall, though, is reluctant to give up on the *Groundwork* definition. He pays lip service to it. He says that the moral requirements that interest him "structure and give expression to the distinctive value that persons equally have: dignity, a 'worth that has no price.'"[43] But I believe that last expression is a wheel that turns nothing in Darwall's account. Everything has to do with the generation of respect through second-person demands. "Worth beyond price" is just decoration.

A more promising approach is indicated in a recent paper by Elizabeth Anderson.[44] Anderson explores the notion of "commanding value," which if it works may bridge the gap between dignity as value-beyond-price and dignity as rank or authority. She is interested in the way Kant appropriated and transformed contemporary ideas about honor: a man of honor treats his independence and self-esteem as something above price; he would not trade it for anything in the world, certainly not for the sake of material interest. This bridges exactly the gap that I am worrying about. And in her view Kant's transformation of it is precisely a universalization of the ethic of honor.[45] If Professor Anderson is right about this, then I should rethink my claim that the famous *Groundwork* definition has little to offer the modern jurisprudence of dignity.

I should repeat that I have no doubt about the importance of the ideas that Kant associates with "dignity" in the *Groundwork* definition: fundamental worth or value beyond price, the insistence that human persons are not to be traded off against each other. But, taken on its own, it has had a deplorable influence on philosophical discussions of dignity and it has led many legal scholars to just assume that "dignity" in the law must convey this specific Kantian resonance.[46] Kant's later work does indeed accord with the idea of dignity as a ranking status. But not the *Groundwork*'s fundamental equation of *Würde* with "value beyond price," at least not without the elaboration that Elizabeth Anderson has offered.

I will have more to say in a moment about conceptions that equate human dignity with the worth or sacred value of human life. Before I do, let me cite one example of the legal use of a Kantian conception of dignity as a simple conception of human worth precluding trade-offs. In a well-known case, the Constitutional Court of Germany considered a statute passed in the wake of the 9/11 terrorist attacks, permitting the German air force to shoot down airliners that had been taken over by terrorists. The German Constitutional Court held that this was not compatible with Article 1 of the Basic Law, which says that "[h]uman dignity is inviolable." Under the Article 1 guarantee of dignity, it is "absolutely inconceivable," said the Court, "to intentionally kill...the crew and the passengers of a hijacked plane, even when they are in a situation that is hopeless for them," that is, even when they are "doomed anyway."[47] "[H]uman dignity," the Court went on, "enjoy[s] the same constitutional protection regardless of the duration of the physical existence of the individual human being." It is an admirable and brave decision, and it may be right. But it takes "dignity" in a direction that leaves behind many of its familiar connotations.

# 7. *Roman Catholic Teaching on Human Dignity*

There are "absolute worth" accounts of dignity and there are "ranking status" accounts. I favor the second, but right now I am trying to do justice to the first, at least in the currency of the scarce time available for this lecture. So here is another well-known conception on the "absolute worth" side of things.

Roman Catholic social teaching about the sanctity of life, about the absolute worth of each human life (starting from conception), and about the absolute character of the prohibitions on murder, abortion, euthanasia, and scientific exploitation of embryos is some-times expressed using the term "dignity."[48] We are told of the "sub-lime" and "almost divine dignity" of every human being, "based on the intimate bond which unites him to his Creator."[49] We are told that "human beings have a special type of *dignity* which is the basis for ... the obligation all of us have not to kill them."[50] This theme is particularly familiar from Roman Catholic doctrine concerning abortion, which cites "the dignity of the unborn child" as the basis for an absolute prohibition on abortion,[51] and holds also that "the use of human embryos or fetuses as an object of experimentation constitutes a crime against their dignity as human beings."[52] What can we make of this?

The view that I take is similar to my view of Kant's definition of *Würde* in the *Groundwork*. I do not understand why "dignity"—with its distinctive connotations—is a good term to use to do work that might be done as well by "worth" or "sacred worth." Having said that, I am quite aware that nothing I say here will persuade Catholics or Kantians to adopt different terminology.

Also, the Catholic account does not altogether ignore alternative approaches to dignity. The sort of conception I am developing in these lectures presents dignity as a rank or status that a person may occupy in society, display in his bearing and self-presentation, and exhibit in his speech and actions. But what about the dignity of those who cannot control their self-presentation or cannot speak up for themselves? John Paul II's encyclical *Evangelium Vitae* con-demns "the mentality which equates personal dignity with a capac-ity for verbal and explicit ... communication."

[O]n the basis of these presuppositions there is no place in the world for anyone who, like the unborn or the dying, is a weak element in the social structure, or for anyone who appears completely at the mercy of others and radically dependent on them, and can only communicate through the silent language of a profound sharing of affection.[53]

The critique is a little overstated. Dignitary provisions, as I understand them, are particularly important for those who are completely at the mercy of others. But I think the former pope was referring to those who are incapable of speaking for themselves or controlling their self-presentation even if they were permitted to: infants and the profoundly disabled. But we should not assume that dignity is the only value in play. I have been at pains to stress that a conception like the one I have been developing does not in any way preclude the independent operation of a principle of the sacred value of all human life.

Certainly we do have to give an account of how human dignity applies to infants and to the profoundly disabled. My own view is that this concern should not necessarily shift us away from a conception that involves the active exercise of a legally defined status. But it does require attention. I believe it can be addressed by the sort of structure that John Locke introduced into his theory of natural rights, when he said of the rank of equality that applies to all humans in virtue of their rationality: "Children, I confess, are not born *in* this full state of equality, though they are born *to* it."[54] Like heirs to an aristocratic title, their present status looks to a rank that they *will* occupy (or are destined to occupy); but it does not require us to invent a different sort of dignity for them in the meantime.

Nothing I have said is intended to refute or cast doubt on the Roman Catholic position regarding the sanctity of life, any more than my critique of Kant casts doubt on his view in the *Groundwork* about trade-offs. We are arguing here about what "dignity" means, not about the permissibility of abortion. And I certainly do not think that any of this shows that dignity (whether in the Catholics' hands or in general) is a stupid or useless concept. Stephen

What about slaves.

Pinker and Ruth Macklin say it does.[55] But they say this just because they are annoyed that Catholics and other "theocons" oppose substantive positions (e.g., about stem-cell experimentation) that Pinker and Macklin support and because they fear that the word "dignity" might intensify that opposition. Pinker and Macklin are not really interested in the analysis of dignity. They oppose the Catholic use of the word because they are politically annoyed by the positions it conveys. They have little interest in what "dignity" might mean if it were not associated with such opposition to abortion or stem-cell research or whatever.

## 8. Rank and Hierarchy

As I have hinted a couple of times, my own view of dignity is that we should contrive to keep faith somehow with its ancient connection to noble rank or high office. In Roman usage, *dignitas* embodied the idea of the honor, the privileges, and the deference due to rank or office,[56] perhaps also reflecting one's distinction in holding that rank or office. Of course Latin *dignitas* does not necessarily equal English "dignity" any more than Kantian *Würde* does. But for the term "dignity" the *Oxford English Dictionary* gives as its second meaning "[h]onourable or high estate, position, or estimation; honour; degree of estimation, rank" and as its third meaning "[a]n honourable office, rank, or title; a high official or titular position."[57]

So people would talk about the dignity of the monarch. A 1690 indictment for high treason against a Jacobite spoke of an "intent to depose the King and Queen, and deprive them of their Royal dignity, and restore the late King James to the government of this kingdom."[58] Blackstone tells us that "the ancient jewels of the Crown are held to be…necessary to maintain the state, and support the dignity, of the sovereign for the time being."[59] And the 1399 statute that took the crown from off the head of Richard II stated that he "renounsed and cessed of the State of Kyng, and of Lordeshipp and of all the Dignite and Wirsshipp that longed therto."[60]

It is not just monarchy. Kant talks about the various dignities of the nobility.[61] In England, nobles had dignity, in the order of duke, marquis, earl, viscount, baron.[62] Degrees have dignity according to law; certainly a doctorate does.[63] Clergymen have dignity, or some do;[64] and a bishop has higher dignity than an abbot.[65] Ambassadors have dignity according to the law of nations.[66] And the French Declaration of the Rights of Man and of the Citizen, approved by the National Assembly in 1789, says in Article 6 that "[a]ll citizens, being equal in the eyes of the law, are equally eligible to all dignities and to all public positions and occupations, according to their abilities, and without distinction except that of their virtues and talents."

Now, this equation of dignity and rank may seem an unpromising idea for human rights discourse, inasmuch as human rights ideology is associated specifically with the *denial* that humans have inherent ranks distinguishing some of them as worthy of special dignity in the way that a duke or a countess might be.[67] However, I am reluctant to leave the matter there. I suspect that this *ranking* sense of "dignity" offers something more to an egalitarian theory of rights than meets the eye.

It might be thought that the old connection between dignity and rank was superseded by a Judeo-Christian notion of the dignity of humanity as such, and that this Judeo-Christian notion is really quite different in character. I am not convinced. I don't want to underestimate the breach between Roman-Greek and Judeo-Christian ideas,[68] but I believe that as far as dignity is concerned the connotation of ranking status remained, and that what happened was that it was transvalued rather than superseded.[69] So let us explore some ways in which the idea of noble rank may be made compatible with an egalitarian conception of dignity.

I said a few moments ago that the Roman Catholic equation of dignity with sacredness of life seems quite different from the idea of dignity as status. Yet when you think about it, the Catholic notion is not unconnected with rank. When we talk about *human* dignity, we may be saying something about rank but not about the rank of some humans over others. We may be talking about rank of humans generally in the great chain of being. The dictionary cites Richard Hooker as writing in *Ecclesiastical Polity* about stones' being "in dignitie of nature inferior to plants."[70] Well, presumably in this ranking, plants are in turn inferior in dignity to beasts, and beasts are inferior to humans, and humans are inferior to angels, and all of them of course are inferior in dignity to God. Catholic dignitary teaching continues to draw on this idea of the special rank accorded to all humans in the great chain of being. Unlike the lower beings, each of us is made in the image of God and each of us bears a special dignity in virtue of that fact.[71]

It is often a striking implication of this sort of ranking that *within* each rank, everything is equal. This has been hugely important for theories of human equality (in John Locke's work, for example).[72] Humans rank higher than other creatures because, with reason and free will, they have God's special favor and are created in his image; this is a rank in which each of us shares, without distinction or discrimination.

Or picture this. In an earlier article on "Dignity and Rank,"[73] I mentioned a certain *transvaluation of values* that seems to have happened in late-eighteenth-century romantic poetry. One begins with an idea of dignity associated with the high rank of some humans (compared to others), and then one *reverses* that ordering ironically or provocatively to claim that the high rank of some is superficial or bogus and that it is the lowly man or the virtues of very ordinary humanity that enjoy true dignity. The *Oxford English Dictionary* cites a passage from William Wordsworth to illustrate this: "True dignity abides with him alone, [w]ho, in the silent hour of inward thought, [c]an still suspect, and still revere himself, [i]n lowliness of heart." But Robert Burns is the real master of this move, with the remarkable reversal of rank/dignity in the three central stanzas of "For A' That and For A' That."

> A prince can mak a belted knight,
> A marquis, duke, an' a' that;
> But an honest man's abon his might,
> Gude faith, he maunna fa' that!
> For a' that, an' a' that,
> Their dignities an' a' that;
> The pith o' sense, an' pride o' worth,
> Are higher rank than a' that.

Burns looks forward to a time when "Sense and Worth, o'er a' the earth, / Shall bear the gree, an' a' that." And then follows the great peroration of human brotherhood, founded on this equality: "For a' that, an' a' that, / It's coming yet for a' that, / That Man to Man, the world o'er, / Shall brothers be for a' that."

The use of "dignity" in this poetry is but an instance of a broader transvaluation that I believe has taken place with regard to dignity generally: a sea change in the way "dignity" is used, enabling it to become a leading concept of *universal* rights (as opposed to special privileges), and bringing into the realm of rights what James Whitman has called "an extension of formerly high-status treatment to all sectors of the population."[74] But we see this only if we understand the *dynamics* of the movement between modern notions of human dignity and an older notion of rank. The older notion is not obliterated; it is precisely the resources of the older notion that are put to work in the new.

So that is my hypothesis: the modern notion of *human* dignity involves an upwards equalization of rank, so that we now try to accord to every human being something of the dignity, rank, and expectation of respect that was formerly accorded to nobility.

## 9. Rank and Equal Rights

Something like this was noticed many years ago by Gregory Vlastos in a neglected essay, "Justice and Equality."[75] In a discussion of equality and rights, Vlastos argued that we organize ourselves not like a society without nobility or rank, but like an aristocratic society that has just one rank (and a pretty high rank at that) for all of us. Or (to vary the image slightly), we are not like a society that has eschewed all talk of caste; we are like a caste society with just one caste (and a very high caste at that). Every man a Brahmin.[76] Every man a duke, every woman a queen, everyone entitled to the sort of deference and consideration, everyone's person and body sacrosanct, in the way that nobles were entitled to deference or in the way that an assault upon the body or the person of a king was regarded as a sacrilege. I take the Vlastos suggestion very seriously indeed. If he is right, then we can use aspects of the traditional meaning of dignity associated with high or noble rank, to cast light on our conceptions of human rights.

Think, for example, of the change that comes when one views an assault on an ordinary man or woman not just as a crude physical interference, but as a sort of sacrilege (like assaulting a prince or a duke). It is a salutary recharacterization of this familiar right, for it reminds us that a dignitarian attitude towards the bodies of others is one of sacral respect, not just nonchalant forbearance. Or think of the proverbial saying "An Englishman's home is his castle." That too reflects something of the generalization of rank. The idea is that we are to live secure in our homes, with all the normative force that a noble's habitation of his ancestral fortress might entail. The modesty of our dwellings does not signify that the right of privacy or security against incursion, search, or seizure is any less momentous.

Or consider, as a third example, the rights of prisoners of war, and the insistence in Common Article 3 of the Geneva Conventions that "outrages upon personal dignity, in particular humiliating and degrading treatment," shall be prohibited. In ages past, chivalry might require that noble warriors, such as knights, be treated with dignity when they fell into the hands of hostile powers; but this was hardly expected in the treatment of the common soldier; they were abused and probably slaughtered. Traces of differential dignity remain: you may remember Colonel Nicholson (played by Alec Guinness) in the David Lean movie *The Bridge on the River Kwai*, who insisted to the Japanese commander of a prisoner-of-war camp that he and his officers were exempt by the laws of war from manual labor, even though the private soldiers under his command might legitimately be forced to work.[77] But modern prohibitions on degrading treatment are oriented specifically to the common soldier, the ordinary detainee, solicitous of their dignity in ways that would have been inconceivable in times past for anyone but officers and gentlemen. (I do not have to remind you how fragile this change is and how close we have come in recent practices of detention in the war on terror to a frightening leveling-down, as we characterize the extension of formerly high-status treatment to all detainees as "quaint and obsolete." I shall say more about these unpleasant realities at the end of my second lecture. For now, it is important to remember that, in these lectures, we are exploring the shape of a *normative* universe, which may or may not succeed in governing or modifying all aspects of our practice. This is as true in law as it is in morality.)

No doubt there are some aristocratic privileges that cannot be universalized, cannot be extended to all men and women. Some we would not want to universalize: a *droit du seigneur*, for example, in matrimonial relations. And some when they are extended will change their character somewhat: a nobleman might insist as a matter of dignity on a right to be consulted, a right to have his voice reckoned with and counted in great affairs of state; if we generalize this—and *really* generalize it—giving *everyone* a right to have his or her voice reckoned with and counted in great affairs of state, then what was formally a high and haughty prerogative might come to seem as mundane as the ordinary democratic vote accorded to tens of millions of citizens. And citizens sometimes complain that their votes are meaningless, and philosophers support them in this complaint.[78] But the dignity hypothesis reminds us that, although it is shared with millions of others, this vote is not a little thing. It too can be understood in a more momentous way, as the entitlement of each person, as part of his or her dignity as an (equal) peer of the realm, to be consulted in public affairs.

I think all this is tremendously helpful in deepening our talk of human dignity and enriching our understanding of rights. The idea that both notions are connected with ideas of status, and with the transvaluation of older notions of rank, is a stimulating one. In my second lecture, I want to say more about the way status works in law, and more too about how the law defines a powerful dignity for us all, in ways that enable us to define a distinctive dignitarian content for the ideal of equality before the law.

## Notes

1. Immanuel Kant, *Groundwork of the Metaphysics of Morals*, in Immanuel Kant, *Practical Philosophy*, ed. Mary Gregor (Cambridge: Cambridge University Press, 1996), at pp. 84–85 (4:435 of the Prussian Academy Edition of Kant's *works*); Stephen Darwall, *The Second-Person Standpoint: Morality, Respect and Accountability* (Cambridge: Harvard University Press, 2006); James Griffin, *On Human Rights* (Oxford: Oxford University Press, 2008).

2. Basic Law (*Grundgesetz*), for the Federal Republic of Germany, Article 1 (1): "Human dignity shall be inviolable. To respect and protect it shall be the duty of all state authority." Constitution of South Africa, Article 10: "Everyone has inherent dignity and the right to have their dignity respected and protected." ICCPR, Article 10 (1): "All persons deprived of their liberty shall be treated with humanity and with respect for the inherent dignity of the human person."

3. A good start, albeit a moderately skeptical one, would be Christopher McCrudden's fine essay, "Human Dignity in Human Rights Interpretation," *European Journal of International Law* 19 (2008): 655–724.

4. For the idea of status in law, see R. H. Graveson, *Status in the Common Law* (London: Athlone Press, 1953). See also the discussion in section 6 of Lecture 2.

5. Much of the argument in this first lecture is based on my essay "Dignity and Rank," *European Journal of Sociology* 48 (2007): 201–37. But I have modified the positions taken in that essay in a number of ways.

6. Wesley N. Hohfeld, *Fundamental Legal Conceptions* (New Haven: Yale University Press, 1919).

7. Even if we say in our model-theoretic conceptions that natural rights precede legal rights in the order of coming-into-being (in Lockean social contract theory, for example), still we should not infer that this corresponds to the order of our understanding of rights, with natural rights being understood first in a way that is independent of any legal understanding.

8. See Ronald Dworkin, *Taking Rights Seriously* (Cambridge: Harvard University Press, 1977).

9. Cf. Oscar Schachter, "Human Dignity as a Normative Concept," *American Journal of International Law* 77 (1983): 848–54, at p. 849: "We do not find an explicit definition of the expression 'dignity of the human person' in international instruments or (as far as I know) in national law. Its intrinsic meaning has been left to intuitive understanding, conditioned in large measure by cultural factors."

10. Joseph Schumpeter, *Capitalism, Socialism and Democracy* (New York: Harper Perennial, 1962), pp. 269 ff.

11. I have pursued this suggestion in Jeremy Waldron, "The Dignity of Groups," *Acta Juridica* (Cape Town) (2009): 66–90, at pp. 68–74.

12. Stephen Pinker thinks it is. In "The Stupidity of Dignity," *New Republic* May 28, 2008, available at http://www.tnr.com/article/the-stupidity-dignity, he complains that the concept "spawns outright contradictions at every turn. We read that slavery and degradation are morally wrong because they take someone's dignity away. But we also read that nothing you can do to a person, including enslaving or degrading him, can take his dignity away."

13. See Jeremy Bentham, *Anarchical Fallacies*, in *Nonsense upon Stilts: Bentham, Burke and Marx on the Rights of Man*, ed. Jeremy Waldron (London: Methuen, 1987), p. 74.

14. Ibid., p. 50.

15. Geneva Conventions, Common Article 3. See also Rome Statute of the International Criminal Court, Article 8 (2) (b) xxi.

16. Constitution of Poland, Article 178(2). The relation between remuneration, subsistence, and dignity is an interesting one. In England it was sometimes held that an impoverished aristocrat could not maintain his dignity. *The Earl of Shrewsbury's Case*, 12 Co. Rep. 106, 77 Eng. Rep. 1383 (1612) cites the terms of an act of Parliament in the reign of Edward IV for the formal degradation of George Nevill, Duke of Bedford: "And forasmuch as it is openly known, that the said George hath not, or by inheritance may have any livelihood to support the same name, estate, and dignity, or any name of estate; and oftentimes it is to be seen, that when any lord is called to high estate, and hath not convenient livelihood to support the same dignity, it…causeth oftentimes great extortion, imbracery and maintenance to be had, to the great trouble of all such countries where such estate shall happen to be: wherefore the King by advice of his Lords Spiritual and Temporal, and by the Commons in this present Parliament assembled,…ordaineth, establisheth, and enacteth, that from henceforth the same creation and making of the said duke, and all the names of dignity given to the said George…be from henceforth void and of none effect."

17. Universal Declaration of Human Rights (1948), Article 23 (3). See also John Locke, *Two Treatises of Government*, ed. Peter Laslett (Cambridge: Cambridge University Press, 1988), p. 277 (II, § 15): "[F]or as much as we are not by ourselves sufficient to furnish ourselves with competent store of things needful for such a life as our Nature doth desire, *a life fit for the dignity of man*, therefore to supply those defects and imperfections which are in us, as living single and solely by ourselves, we are naturally induced to seek communion and fellowship with others" (my emphasis).

18. See also Daniel Statman, "Humiliation, Dignity, and Self-Respect," in *The Concept of Human Dignity in Human Rights Discourse*, ed. David Kretzmer and Eckart Klein (New York: Kluwer Law Interna-

tional, 2002): 209–29, p. 209: "Tying the concept of humiliation to that of human dignity makes the former too philosophical…and too detached from psychological research and theory."

19. The Universal Declaration of Human Rights (Article 5) and the ICCPR (Article 7) both provide that "[n]o one shall be subjected to torture or to cruel, inhuman, or degrading treatment or punishment."

20. Hannah Arendt, *On Revolution* (Harmondsworth: Penguin, 1977), p. 278.

21. Griffin, *On Human Rights*, p. 31, drawing on Giovanni Pico della Mirandola, *Oration on the Dignity of Man* (1486), available at http://cscs.umich.edu/~crshalizi/Mirandola/.

22. Griffin, *On Human Rights*, p. 152.

23. Ibid., pp. 179–80.

24. Ibid., pp. 149 ff.

25. See Jan Robert Bloch and Caspers Rubin, "How Can We Understand the Bends in the Upright Gait?" *New German Critique* 45 (1988): 9–39, at pp. 9–10.

26. See also the account in Aurel Kolnai, "Dignity," *Philosophy* 51 (1976): 251–71, at pp. 253–54.

27. See Jeremy Waldron, "Cruel, Inhuman, and Degrading Treatment: The Words Themselves," *Canadian Journal of Law and Jurisprudence* 23 (2010): 269–86 (also in Jeremy Waldron, *Torture, Terror, and Trade-Offs* [New York: Oxford University Press, 2010]: 276–319) for the ways in which the bestialization or infantilization of detainees is at odds with this (in the "war on terror").

28. Ronald Dworkin, *Is Democracy Possible Here?* (Princeton: Princeton University Press, 2008), p. 9. The account is greatly expanded in Ronald Dworkin, *Justice for Hedgehogs* (Cambridge: Harvard University Press, 2010), pp. 191–218 *et passim*.

29. Dworkin, *Is Democracy Possible Here?* p. 10.

30. It is interesting that in his early work on rights, Dworkin distinguished his own position, which he articulated in terms of equality, from positions that he called Kantian, which were associated with dignity: see Dworkin, *Taking Rights Seriously*, pp. 198–99.

31. Cf. Lewis Carroll, *Through the Looking Glass, and What Alice Found There* (Philadelphia: Henry Altemus, 1899), p. 123.

32. Kant, *Groundwork*, pp. 84–85 (4:435 of the Prussian Academy Edition of Kant's works). Kant goes on to say that the moral will is "infinitely above all price." He says it cannot be brought into comparison or competition with any other value at all "without, as it were, assaulting its holiness." Notice also that James Griffin is wary of associating his view with Kantian dignity; he says that dignity in the Kantian sense is supposed to be characteristic of all morality, not just human rights (Griffin, *On Human Rights*, p. 201).

33. For a suggestive discussion of some differences, see Kolnai, "Dignity," at pp. 251–52. See also the comment in *Dignity—Ethics and Law: Bibliography* (Copenhagen: Centre for Ethics and Law, 1999), p. 9: "The Scandinavian and German nouns *vœdighed* and *Würde* are derived from the Germanic *werpa- (werd, wert)* which means that these languages point to worth and value more than to dignity."

34. McCrudden, "Human Dignity in Human Rights Interpretation," at p. 679, follows Gerald Neuman, "Human Dignity in United States Constitutional Law," in *Zur Autonomie des Individuums: Liber Amicorum Spiros Simitis*, ed. D. Simon and M. Weiss (Baden-Baden: Nomos, 2000), at pp. 249–50, in identifying the core meaning of "human dignity" with the intrinsic *worth* of the individual.

35. Kolnai's discussion of this in "Dignity," at pp. 252–54, is very fine.

36. Kantian respect, important though it is in his moral philosophy, is not really the right sort of shape for our purposes. In the Second Critique, Kant presents respect as a feeling of awe that a person experiences when he notices how pure practical reason strikes down his inclinations and his self-conceit. (See Immanuel Kant, *Critique of Practical Reason*, Part I, ch. 3, in *Practical Philosophy*, pp. 199 ff. [5:73 ff.].) It is like amazement and admiration that there should be this moral capacity, a response that I have to my own sense of duty. It is not independently a way of generating duties. Kant himself seems to recognize this because, as he puts it, "the concept of duty cannot be derived from respect" (ibid., p. 172 (5:38). Kant used the term "respect" very carefully. We tend to use it quite loosely, and we may be seeing in his account not what it strictly implies but what we need.

37. See Michel Rosen, "'The Shibboleth of All Empty-Headed Moralists': The Place of Dignity in Ethics and Politics," 2007 Boston University

Benedict Lectures, now published as Dignity: Its History and Meaning (Cambridge: Harvard University Press, 2012).

38. In the *Critique of Practical Reason*, p. 200 (5:74), Kant says: "If something represented as a determining ground of our will humiliates us in our self-consciousness, it awakens respect for itself insofar as it is a positive and a determining ground. Therefore the moral law is even subjectively a ground of respect."

39. Immanuel Kant, *The Metaphysics of Morals*, in *Practical Philosophy*, pp. 470–72 (6:328–30).

40. Ibid., pp. 558–59 (6:436).

41. Ibid., pp. 557–58 (6:435–36): "[F]rom our capacity for internal lawgiving and from the (natural) human being's feeling himself compelled to revere the (moral) human being within his own person, at the same time there comes exaltation of the highest self-esteem, the feeling of his inner worth, in terms of which he is above any price and possesses an inalienable dignity, which instills in him respect for himself."

42. Darwall, *The Second-Person Standpoint*, ch. 6.

43. Ibid., p. 119.

44. See Elizabeth Anderson, "Emotions in Kant's Later Moral Philosophy: Honor and the Phenomenology of Moral Value," in *Kant's Ethics of Virtue*, ed. Monika Betzler (New York: de Gruyter, 2008): 123–46.

45. Ibid., p. 139: "The ethic of honor reserves respect, the status of being a bearer of commanding value…exclusively to people of superior social rank. [But] Kant's ethic universalizes respectful standing to all rational agents."

46. See, for example, Stephen J. Heyman, *Free Speech and Human Dignity* (New Haven: Yale University Press, 2008), p. 39, simply defining dignity as "near absolute worth." See also Schachter, "Human Dignity as a Normative Concept," p. 849, equating dignity with "the Kantian injunction to treat every human being as an end not as a means," and G. P. Fletcher, "Human Dignity as a Constitutional Value," *University of Western Ontario Law Review* 22 (1984): 171–82.

47. *Bundesverfassungsgericht*, February 15, 2006, 115 BVerfGE 118, available at http://www.bundesverfassungsgericht.de/en/decisions/rs200 60215_1bvr035705en.html. "[T]he assessment that the persons who are on board a plane that is intended to be used against other people's

lives...are doomed anyway cannot remove its nature of an infringement of their right to dignity from the killing of innocent people in a situation that is desperate for them which an operation performed pursuant to this provisions as a general rule involves. Human life and human dignity enjoy the same constitutional protection regardless of the duration of the physical existence of the individual human being....Whoever denies this or calls this into question denies those who, such as the victims of a hijacking, are in a desperate situation that offers no alternative to them, precisely the respect which is due to them for the sake of their human dignity."

48. See Pope John Paul II's encyclical *Evangelium Vitae* (March 25, 1995), available at http://www.vatican.va/holy_father/john_paul_ii/encyclicals/documents/hf_jp-ii_enc_25031995_evangelium-vitae_en.html.

49. Ibid., §§ 25, 34, and 38.

50. Patrick Lee and Robert George, "The Nature and Basis of Human Dignity," *Ratio Juris* 21 (2008): 173.

51. *Evangelium Vitae*, § 44.

52. Ibid., §63. For discussion, see also *Human Dignity and Bioethics: Essays Commissioned by the President's Council on Bioethics* (Washington D.C., 2008), available at http://www.bioethics.gov/reports/human_ dignity /index.html.

53. *Evangelium Vitae*, § 19.

54. Locke, *Two Treatises*, p. 304 (II, § 55).

55. Stephen Pinker says that "'dignity' is a squishy, subjective notion, hardly up to the heavyweight moral demands assigned to it." He adds: "The sickness in theocon bioethics [involves] imposing a Catholic agenda on a secular democracy and using 'dignity' to condemn anything that gives someone the creeps." See Pinker, "The Stupidity of Dignity" and also Ruth Macklin, "Editorial: Dignity Is a Useless Concept," *British Medical Journal* 327 (2003): 1419–20, at p. 1420.

56. See Teresa Iglesias, "Bedrock Truths and the Dignity of the Individual," *Logos: A Journal of Catholic Thought and Culture* 4 (2001): 114–34, at pp. 120–21: "The idea of *dignitas* was central to Roman political and social life and closely related to the meaning of honor. Political offices, and as a consequence the persons holding them, like that of a senator, or the emperor, had *dignitas*."

57. Samuel Johnson defined dignity as "a rank of elevation" in *A Dictionary of the English Language*, cited by Michael Meyer in "Dignity as a (Modern) Virtue," in Kretzmer and Klein, *The Concept of Human Dignity*: 195–207, at p. 196.

58. *Patrick Harding's Case*, 86 Eng. Rep. 461, 2 Ventris, 315. And a felony would be said to be committed "against the peace of our…Lord the King, his crown and dignity."

59. Wayne Morrison, ed., *Blackstone's Commentaries on the Laws of England* (London: Cavendish Publishing, 2001), 2:347 (ch. 28).

60. 1399 Rolls Parl. III. 424/1, as cited in the *Oxford English Dictionary's* entry for "dignity."

61. Kant, *Metaphysics of Morals*, p. 471 (6:330).

62. Morrison, *Blackstone's Commentaries on the Laws of England*, 1:30–35 (ch. 12).

63. *Doctor Bentley's Case*, 92 Eng. Rep. 818, Fortescue, 202 (1737).

64. Though not all holy orders are technically dignities. See Boughton v. Gousley, Cro. Eliz. 663 78 Eng. Rep. 901 (1599): "The civilians divided spiritual functions into three degrees. First, a function, which hath a jurisdiction; as bishop, dean, &c. Secondly, a spiritual administration, with a cure; as parson of a church, &c. Thirdly, they who have neither cure nor jurisdiction; as prebends, chaplains, &c. And they defined a dignity to be *administratio ecclesiastica cum jurisdictione, vel potestate conjunctd*, and thereby they exclude the two last degrees from being any dignity;…an archdeacon is not a name of dignity:…a parson is not a name of dignity.…a provost is not a name of dignity.…a precentor is not a name of dignity.…a chaplain is not a name of dignity."

65. *Cootes v. Atkinson*, 75 Eng. Rep. 1072, Gouldsborough, 171.

66. *Taylor v. Best*, 139 Eng. Rep. 201, 14 C. B. 487.

67. In America, for example, we associate the egalitarian rights-talk of (say) the opening lines of the Declaration of Independence with the Constitution's insistence in Article 1: 9 (viii) that "[n]o title of nobility shall be granted by the United States."

68. See, for example, Joshua A. Berman, *Created Equal: How the Bible Broke with Ancient Political Thought* (Oxford: Oxford University Press, 2008).

69. Even those who think in terms of a fundamental opposition be-tween the rank notion of dignity and the human rights notion of dignity also discern a dynamic connection. Iglesias, "Bedrock Truths," p. 120, dis-tinguishes between what she calls the universal and the restricted mean-ings of dignity. She writes: "Consulting the dictionary we can find that the term 'dignity' connotes 'superiority,' and the 'decorum' relating to it, in two basic senses. One refers to superiority of role either in rank, office, excellence, power, etc., which can pertain only to *some* human beings....The other refers to the superiority of intrinsic worth of every human being that is independent of external conditions of office, rank, etc. and that pertains to *everyone*. In this universal sense the word 'dignity' captures the mode of being specific to the human being *as* a human being. This latter meaning, then, has a universal and uncondi-tional significance, in contrast with the former that is restrictive and role-determined." Iglesias associates the restrictive use with classical Roman culture and the universal use with notions of inherent human worth that emerged in Jewish ethics and theology. But though, as she says, "the meaning of dignity has been historically marked, up to the present time, by a tension between its universal and its restrictive mean-ings," what has happened is that "historically, the restrictive Roman meaning of *dignitas* assigned to office and rank, and used as a discrimina-tory legal measure, began to be used with a new meaning of universal significance that captures the equal worth of everyone" (p. 122).

70. The OED citation is as follows: "1594 HOOKER Eccl. Pol. I. vi. (1611) 12 Stones, though in dignitie of nature inferior to plants."

71. See Jeremy Waldron, "The Image of God: Rights, Reason, and Order," in *Christianity and Human Rights: An Introduction*, ed. John Witte and Frank Alexander (New York: Cambridge University Press, 2010).

72. Locke, *Two Treatises*, pp. 269–71(II, §§ 4 and 6) wrote that there is "nothing more evident, than that creatures of the same species and rank, promiscuously born to all the same advantages of nature, and the use of the same faculties, should also be equal one amongst another without subordination or subjection...[B]eing furnished with like facul-ties,...there cannot be supposed any such subordination among us that may authorise us to destroy one another, as if we were made for one another's uses, as the inferior ranks of creatures are for ours."

73. Waldron, "Dignity and Rank," p. 220.

74. James Whitman, "Human Dignity in Europe and the United States: The Social Foundations," in *Europe and US Constitutionalism*, ed. G. Nolte (New York: Cambridge University Press, 2005): 108–24, at p. 110 argues that "[t]he core idea of 'human dignity' in Continental Europe is that old forms of low-status treatment are no longer acceptable....'Human dignity,' as we find it on the Continent today, has been formed by a pattern of leveling up, an extension of formerly high-status treatment to all sectors of the population."

75. Gregory Vlastos, "Justice and Equality," in *Theories of Rights*, ed. Jeremy Waldron (New York: Oxford University Press, 1984): 41–76.

76. Ibid., p. 54. Vlastos continues: "To reproduce this feature of our system we would have to look not only to caste-societies, but to extremely rigid ones, since most of them make some provision for elevation in rank for rare merit or degradation for extreme demerit....And the fact that first-class citizenship, having been made common, is no longer a mark of distinction does not trivialize the privileges it entails. It is the simple truth, not declamation, to speak of it, as I have done, as a 'rank of dignity' in some ways comparable to that enjoyed by hereditary nobilities of the past."

77. David Lean, *The Bridge on the River Kwai* (Columbia Pictures, 1957). Colonel Nicholson clearly believes that forcing the officers to work would be degrading, and he suffers a great deal as a result of the Japanese reaction to his refusal to accept this degrading treatment. Intriguing though this is, however, it is pretty clear that the reference to degrading treatment in the modern Geneva Conventions is not about insensitivity to military rank. It depends on an idea of dignity that is more egalitarian than that.

78. Benjamin Constant, "The Liberty of the Ancients Compared with that of the Moderns," in *Constant: Political Writings*, ed. Biancamaria Fontana (Cambridge: Cambridge University Press, 1988): 307–28, at p. 316, gives voice to this concern when he contrasts the participatory rights of the ancients with those of modern suffrage: "The share which in antiquity everyone held in national sovereignty was by no means an abstract presumption as it is in our own day. The will of each individual had real influence: the exercise of this will was a vivid and repeated pleasure....This compensation no longer exists for us today. Lost in the

multitude, the individual can almost never perceive the influence he exercises. Never does his will impress itself upon the whole; nothing confirms in his eyes his own cooperation." But maybe the better view is that of Judge Learned Hand, quoted in Dworkin, *Freedom's Law: The Moral Reading of the American Constitution* (Cambridge: Harvard University Press, 1996), p. 343, who contemplated the possibility of being "ruled by a bevy of Platonic Guardians":

> I should miss the stimulus of living in a society where I have, at least theoretically, some part in the direction of public affairs. Of course I know how illusory would be the belief that my vote determined anything; but nevertheless when I go to the polls I have a satisfaction in the sense that we are all engaged in a common venture. If you retort that a sheep in the flock may feel something like it; I reply, following Saint Francis, "My brother, the Sheep."

# Lecture 2: Law, Dignity, and Self-Control

In the first lecture, I toyed with the idea that "dignity" is a term used to indicate a high-ranking legal, political, and social status, and that the idea of *human* dignity is the idea of the assignment of such a high-ranking status to everyone. We know that human dignity can be treated as a moral concept. But I was also pursuing a hunch that we might do better by considering first how dignity works as a legal concept—and then model what we want to do with it morally on that. I argued that we should consider ways in which the idea of human dignity keeps faith with the old hierarchical system of dignity as noble or official rank and that we should view it in its modern form as an equalization of high status rather than as something that eschews talk of status altogether. In my second lecture, I want to pursue this further by considering the variety of ways in which law vindicates dignity in this sense.

## 1. Protecting Status

Historically law has done all sorts of things to protect and vindicate dignity in the sense of rank or high status. English law protected nobles against imputations against their dignity by the offense (and tort) of *scandalum magnatum*.[1] It also protected the exclusiveness of rank with things like sumptuary laws, and requirements of proper address, deference, privilege, and precedence. If I am right that dignity is still the name of a rank—only now an equally distributed one—and that this is a different matter from there being no rank at all in the law, then we would expect modern law also to commit itself to protection and vindication of the high rank or dignity of the ordinary person. And so it does, in various ways.

We have seen that law tries to protect individuals against treatment that is degrading.[2] That is one very elementary way in which law protects dignity. Another is protection from insult—a sort of democratized *scandalum magnatum*. In countries where hate speech and group libel are prohibited, people are required to refrain from the most egregious public attacks on one another's basic social standing. A great many countries use their laws to protect ethnic and racial groups from threatening, abusive, or insulting publications calculated to bring them into public contempt.[3] The United States is an exception in the latitude it currently gives to hate speech; but even here the notion of a dignitarian basis for banning hate speech is often cited in the constitutional debate, where it is understood as posing a freedom-versus-dignity dilemma.[4] Elsewhere these restrictions are not widely viewed as violations of individual rights; most countries say they have enacted them pursuant to their obligations under the International Covenant on Civil and Political Rights, which says that expressions of hatred likely to stir up violence, hostility, or discrimination *must* be prohibited by law.[5]

The other way that law protects dignity is by prohibiting invidious discrimination. This has been very important in South African jurisprudence.[6] According to the Constitutional Court, the history of the country demonstrates that discrimination "proceeds on [an] assumption that the disfavoured group is inferior to other groups. And this is an assault on the human dignity of the disfavoured group." The Court went on: "Equality as enshrined in our Constitution does not tolerate distinctions that treat other people as 'second class citizens.'"[7]

A similar approach has been taken in Canada. In a 1999 decision, it was said that "the purpose of [the antidiscrimination provisions of the Canadian Charter of Rights and Freedoms] is to prevent the violation of essential human dignity…through the imposition of disadvantage, stereotyping, or political or social prejudice, and to promote a society in which all persons enjoy equal recognition at law as human beings or as members of Canadian society, equally capable and equally deserving of concern, respect and consideration."[8] The Canadian court said that this "overriding concern" with dignity infuses all elements of the discrimination analysis and it figured that dignitarian ideas could be used to distinguish between invidious and benign discrimination.[9]

Mostly in this lecture I want to talk about some less obvious ways in which law protects dignity—ways, though, that are more pervasive and more intimately connected with the very nature of law. For when we think about something like Common Article 3 of the Geneva Conventions, it may strike us as a matter of contingency that dignity is protected in this way; we have seen in recent years how fragile the Geneva Conventions are. Or consider that in 2008, the Supreme Court of Canada decided it would no longer use dignity as the touchstone of its antidiscrimination doctrine.[10] It was persuaded by some academic writing that "human dignity is an abstract and subjective notion" that is "confusing and difficult to apply."[11] So it turned its back on dignity as the basis of antidiscrimination doctrine. Courts do that sometimes. They just decide to change the basis and direction of doctrine. Are there connections between law and dignity that are less contingent than this?

## 2. The Dignity of Being a Right-Bearer

One possibility is that even if jurisdictions vary in their readiness to acknowledge specific dignitary rights, still the very form and structure of a right conveys the idea of the right-bearer's dignity. Right-bearers stand up for themselves; they make unapologetic claims on their own behalf; they control the pursuit and prosecution of their own grievances. In the words of Alan Gewirth, the ultimate purpose of rights

is to secure for each person a certain fundamental moral status: that of having rational autonomy and dignity in the sense of being a self-controlling, self-developing agent who can relate to other persons on a basis of mutual respect and cooperation, in contrast to being a dependent, passive recipient of the agency of others.[12]

Rights reek of dignity, particularly in H. L. A. Hart's "choice theory" of rights, for example.[13] Hart was convinced that having a legal or a moral right was not just a matter of being the object of legal or moral concern; he rejected what is sometimes known as the "benefit theory" of rights associated with Jeremy Bentham. He favored instead the description of the right-bearer as having the power to determine what another's duty should be (in some regard):

Y is...in a position to determine by his choice how X shall act and in this way to limit X's freedom of choice; and it is this fact, not the fact that he stands to benefit, that makes it appropriate to say that he has a right.[14]

Y (the right-bearer) can make a sort of demand upon X that X and the institutions of the law are required to pay attention to, and it may be that this is what Y's dignity amounts to. Hart developed this argument first for natural rights, but he thought (at least for a while) that it was true of legal rights too.[15]

Something similar can be found in Joel Feinberg's work on rights as claims: to have a right in law is to possess the dignity of a recognized claimant entitled to push his case before us and demand that it be considered.[16] A right, he says, is something that can be "demanded, claimed, insisted upon without embarrassment or shame."[17] Indeed Feinberg suggests that "what is called 'human dignity' may simply be the recognizable capacity to assert claims."[18] To the extent that rights are pervasive in law, the recognition and respect that claimants are entitled to elicit is going to be a pervasive aspect of law's commitment to dignity.

It is sometimes said that we can imagine law without rights. If that means we can imagine law without any of the elements discussed in this section, I think it is false. Even if Hart and Feinberg are wrong about rights generally, law will nevertheless characteristically (not just contingently) establish and respect positions that have the features that their theories attributed to rights: for example, law will recognize potential plaintiffs and defer to their dignity in allowing *them* to make the decision whether some norm-violator is to be taken to task or not. It is even more evidently false if Ronald Dworkin is right in the basic "rights thesis" he set out years ago in *Taking Rights Seriously*. Dworkin argued that anyone making a case of any sort in law makes it in the tones and language of rights, in the mode of entitlement rather than request or lobbying. A party in law does not phrase his argument in terms of its being *a rather good idea* to require a defendant or respondent to pay such and such a sum of money; he stands on his rights and in recognizing this standing the law accords him the dignity of a right-bearer.

## 3. Dignity and the "Inner Morality" of Law

What about other internal connections between dignity and the forms and procedures of law? Well, we are familiar with something like this in the contrast between internal and external aspects of law's moral connections in the jurisprudence of Lon Fuller.

In his book *The Morality of Law*, Fuller developed an account of what he called the inner morality of law—the formal principles of generality, prospectivity, clarity, stability, consistency, whose observance is bound up with the basics of legal craftsmanship.[19] Legal positivists have sometimes expressed bewilderment as to why Fuller called these internal principles a "morality."[20] He did so because he thought his eight principles had inherent moral significance. It was not only that he believed that observing them made it much more difficult to do substantive injustice; though this he did believe. It was also because he thought observing the principles he identified was itself a way of respecting human dignity:

> To embark on the enterprise of subjecting human conduct to rules involves...a commitment to the view that man is...a responsible agent, capable of understanding and following rules....Every departure from the principles of law's inner morality is an affront to man's dignity as a responsible agent. To judge his actions by unpublished or retrospective laws, or to order him to do an act that is impossible, is to convey...your indifference to his powers of self-determination.[21]

These are not just platitudes. Fuller is referring here to a quite specific characteristic of law—its general reliance on what Henry Hart and Albert Sacks in *The Legal Process* called "self-application," people applying officially promulgated norms to their own conduct, rather than waiting for coercive intervention from the state.[22] Self-application is an important feature of the way legal systems operate. They work by using, rather than short-circuiting, the agency of ordinary human individuals. They count on people's capacities for practical understanding, self-control, self-monitoring, and the modulation of their own behavior in regard to norms that they can grasp and understand. All this makes ruling by law quite different from (say) herding cows with a cattle prod or directing a flock of sheep with a dog. It is quite different too from eliciting a reflex recoil with a scream of command. A pervasive emphasis on self-application is, in my view, definitive of law, distinguishing it sharply from systems of rule that work primarily by manipulating, terrorizing, or galvanizing behavior.[23]

In an article published some years ago, Michael Meyer argued for a strong link between human dignity and the idea of self-control.[24] Meyer emphasized mainly the self-control involved in one's self-presentation to others. We talked about this in my first lecture, in regard to the noble bearing and self-possession that dignity expresses and protects. But self-command is more than just *setting one's stance*, as it were. It is also a matter of people fine-tuning their behavior effectively and gracefully in response to the legitimate demands that may be made upon them, controlling external behavior—monitoring it and modulating it in accordance with one's understanding of a norm.[25] This one might imagine as quintessentially aristocratic virtue, a form of self-command distinguished from the behavior of those who need to be driven by threats or the lash, or by forms of habituation that depend upon threats and the lash. But if it is an aristocratic virtue, it is one that law now expects to find in all sectors of the population.

One other point in this regard. Law does not always present itself to us as a set of crisply defined rules that are meant to be obeyed mechanically. Its demands often come to us in the form of standards—like the standard of "reasonable care"—norms that require, frame, and facilitate genuine thought in the way we receive and comply with them.

Some may wonder whether law can guide conduct (and be self-applying) if the indeterminacy of standards is not reduced to clear rules through official elaboration. But in many areas of life, law proceeds without such definitive elaboration. We operate on the basis that it is sometimes better to facilitate thoughtfulness about a certain type of situation ("When there is fog, drive at a *reasonable* speed") than to lay down an operationalized rule ("When visibility is reduced to less than a hundred meters, lower your speed by fifteen miles per hour"). And people respond to this. If standards rely necessarily on official elaboration, then the life of the law shows that ordinary people can sometimes have the dignity of judges. They do their own elaborations. They are their own officials: they recognize a norm, they apprehend its bearing on their conduct, and they make a determination and act on it.

## 4. Hearings and Due Process

Another way in which law respects the dignity of those who are governed is in the provision that it makes for hearings in cases where an official determination is necessary. These are cases where self-application is not possible or where there is a dispute that requires official resolution. By hearings, I mean formal events, like trials, tightly structured in a procedural way in order to enable an impartial tribunal to determine rights and responsibilities fairly and effectively after hearing evidence and argument from both sides. Those who are immediately concerned have an opportunity to make submissions and present evidence, and confront, examine, and respond to evidence and submissions presented from the other side. Not only that, but both sides are listened to by a tribunal that is bound to respond to the arguments put forward in the reasons that it eventually gives for its decision.[26]

Law, we can say, is a mode of governance that acknowledges that people likely have a view or perspective of their own to present on the application of a social norm to their conduct. Applying a norm to a human individual is not like deciding what to do about a rabid animal or a dilapidated house. It involves paying attention to a point of view. In this way it embodies a crucial dignitarian idea—respecting the dignity of those to whom the norms are applied as beings capable of explaining themselves.

The institutional character of law makes law a matter of argument, and this contributes yet another strand to law's respect for human dignity. Law presents itself as something one can make sense of. The norms that are administered in our legal system may seem like just one damned command after another, but lawyers and judges try to see the law as a whole; to discern some sort of coherence or system, integrating particular items into a structure that makes intellectual sense. And ordinary people take advantage of this aspiration to systematicity and integrity in framing their own legal arguments—by inviting the tribunal hearing their case to consider how the position they are putting forward fits generally into a coherent conception of the spirit of the law.

As we noticed in our reference to the rights thesis, these are not just arguments about what the law *ought to be*—made, as it were, in a sort of lobbying mode. They are arguments of reason presenting competing arguments about what the law is. Inevitably, they are controversial: one party will say that such-and-such a proposition cannot be inferred from the law as it is; the other party will respond that it can be so inferred if only we credit the law with more coherence (or coherence among more of its elements) than people have tended to credit it with in the past. And so the determination of whether such a proposition has legal authority may often be a matter of contestation.[27]

In this way too, then, law conceives of the people who live under it as bearers of reason and intelligence. They are thinkers who can grasp and grapple with the rationale of the way they are governed and relate it in complex but intelligible ways to their own view of the relation between their actions and purposes and the actions and purposes of the state. This too is a tribute to human dignity.

## 5. Legal Hierarchy and Legal Equality

For us, dignity and equality are interdependent.[28] But one can imagine (or historically one can recall) systems of governance that involved a radical discrimination, in legal standing, among individuals of different ranks. High-ranking persons might be regarded as capable of participating fully in something like a legal system: they would be trusted with the voluntary self-application of norms; their word and testimony would be taken seriously; they would be entitled to the benefit of elaborate processes, and so on. Also among high-ranking persons, there might be important distinctions of which law applies. Those with a certain high dignity used to have the right to be tried according to a separate system of law. For example, nobles used to be entitled to trial by their peers or by the House of Lords (as a court of first instance), certainly not by a common jury.[29] Or you might be unable to proceed against a duke or a baron for debt, in the ordinary way.

Consider this example. In 1606, in London, a carriage carrying Isabel, the Countess of Rutland, was attacked by serjeants-at-mace pursuant to a writ alleging a debt of £1,000.

[T]he said serjeants in Cheapside, with many others, came to the countess in her coach, and shewed her their mace, and touching her body with it, said to her, we arrest you, madam, at the suit of the [creditor]…and thereupon they compelled the coachman to carry the said countess to the compter in Wood Street,…where she remained seven or eight days, till she paid the debt.[30]

The Star Chamber held that the "arrest of the countess by the serjeants-at-mace…is against law, and the said countess was falsely imprisoned" and "a severe sentence was given against [the creditor], the serjeants, and the others their confederates." The court quoted an ancient maxim to the effect that "law will have a difference between a lord or a lady, &c. and another common person," and it held that "the person of one who is…a countess by marriage, or by descent, is not to be arrested for debt or trespass; for although in respect of her sex she cannot sit in Parliament, yet she is a peer of the realm, and shall be tried by her peers." There are two reasons, the court went on, "why her person should not be arrested in such cases; one in respect of her dignity, and the other in respect that the law doth presume that she hath sufficient lands and tenements in which she may be distrained."[31] In light of this presumption of noble wealth, the seizing of her body cannot legally be justified as it could in those days to recover the debts of a commoner. Since then, however, things have changed. Now we apply this noble presumption to all debtors: we may not assume their wealth as the English court assumed the countess's, but we accord them the same dignity. And in light of that, *no one's* body is allowed to be seized; no one can be held or imprisoned for debt.

At the other extreme, in our imagined (or recollected) hierarchical society, there might be a caste or class of persons, who were dealt with purely coercively by the authorities. There would be no question of trusting them or anything they said; they would appear in shackles if they appeared in a hearing at all; like slaves in ancient Athens, their evidence would be required to be taken under torture; and they would not be entitled to make decisions or arguments relating to their own defense, nor to have their statements heard or taken seriously. They would not necessarily be entitled to bring suit in the courts, or if they were it would have to be under someone else's protection; they would not be, as we sometimes say, *sui juris*. Slave societies were like that, and many other societies in the past, with which we are uncomfortably familiar, evolved similar discriminating forms that distinguished between (for example) the legal dignity of a noble, the legal dignity of a common man, the legal dignity of a woman, and the legal dignity of a slave, serf, or villein.

I think it is part of our modern notion of law that almost all such gross status differences have been abandoned (though there are relics here and there). We have adopted the idea of a single-status system,[32] evolving a more or less universal status—a more or less universal legal dignity—that entitles everyone to something like the treatment before law that was previously confined to high-status individuals.

## 6. Sortal and Condition Status

I have said that dignity should be considered as a status. It is time to pause and reflect on this idea. Legal status has been defined by one jurist, R. S. Graveson, as a special condition of a continuous and institutional nature, differing from the legal position of the normal person, which is conferred by law…whenever a person occupies a position of which the creation, continuance or relinquishment and the incidents thereof are a matter of sufficient social concern.[33]

The monarch has distinctive powers; a bankrupt has distinctive disabilities; serving members of the armed forces have distinctive duties and distinctive privileges; and so on.[34]

I disagree with the claim, implicit in Graveson's definition ("a special condition…differing from the legal position of the normal person"), that there is no such thing as ordinary legal status. I am not sure why he says this, and I will explain why I disagree in a moment.

Before I do, I would like to introduce an elementary distinction between two types of status—*sortal* status and *condition* status, to elaborate what I am saying about a dignitarian society being, these days, a single-status society. (I base the terminology on the beginning of an intercession in the old Book of Common Prayer for "all sorts and conditions of men.")[35]

Let us begin with condition status. Some distinctions of status are still with us. There are legal statuses that apply to individuals in virtue of certain conditions they are in, that they may not be in forever, or that they may have fallen into by choice or happenstance: they embody the more important legal consequences of some of the ordinary stages of human life (infancy, minority), or some of the choices people make (marriage, felony, military service, being an alien), or some of the vicissitudes that ordinary humanity is heir to (lunacy) or that through bad luck or bad management may afflict one's ordinary dealings with others (bankruptcy, for example). I call these condition statuses. They tell us nothing about the underlying personhood of the individuals who have them: they arise out of conditions into which anyone might fall.

Condition status may be contrasted with sortal status. Sortal status categorizes legal subjects on the basis of *the sort of person* they are. One's sortal status defines a sort of baseline (relative to condition status). Modern notions of sortal status are hard to find, but earlier I mentioned a few historical examples: villeinage and slavery. Racist legal systems such as that of apartheid era South Africa or American law from 1776 until (at least) 1867 recognized sortal statuses based on race. Some legal systems ascribe separate status to women. Sortal status represents a person's permanent situation and destiny so far as the law is concerned. It is not acquired or lost depending on actions, growth, circumstances, or vicissitudes. The idea behind sortal status is that there are different kinds of person.

Now it is precisely this last claim that the principle of *human dignity* denies. There are not different kinds of person, at least not for human persons.[36] We once thought that there were different kinds of human—slaves and free; women and men; commoners and nobles; black and white—and that it was important, from a social point of view, that there be public determination and control of the respective rights, duties, powers, liabilities, and immunities associated with personhood of each kind. We no longer think this. There is basically just one kind of human person in the eyes of the law, and condition status is defined by contrast with this baseline.

But *what kind* of person is that? What is the baseline of sortal status? We used to think there were many kinds: nobles, commoners, slaves, and so on. Which one have we made standard? The idea I pursued at the end of Lecture 1 is that we have made standard a rather high-ranking status, high enough to be termed a "dignity." The standard status for people now is more like an earldom than like the status of a peasant; more like a knight than a squire. Or forget the quaint Blackstonian conceits: it is more like the status of a free man than like a slave or bondsman; it is more like the status of a person who is *sui juris* than the status of a subject who needs someone to speak for him; it is the status of a right-bearer—the bearer of an imposing array of rights—rather than the status of someone who mostly labors under duties; it is the status of someone who can demand to be heard and taken into account; it is more like the status of someone who issues commands than like the status of someone who merely obeys them.

Of course it is an equal status. We are all chiefs; there are no Indians. If we all—each of us—issue commands or demand to be taken seriously or insist on speaking for ourselves, it is everyone else—all of us, our peers, who have similar standing—who have to obey or make room or listen. But this does not mean that we might as well all be peasants or squires or bondsmen. High status can be universalized and still remain high, as each of an array of millions of people regards him- or herself (and all of the others) as a locus of respect, as a self-originating source of legal and moral claims. We all stand proud, and—if I may be permitted a paradox—we all look up to each other from a position of upright equality. I am not saying we always keep faith with this principle. But that is the shape of the principle of dignity that we're committed to. (And that, incidentally, is why I insisted, against Graveson, that we should be able to draw attention to the distinctive features of ordinary sortal status among us, even when there is no special sortal status to contrast it with.)

If I were to give a name the status I have in mind, the high rank or dignity attributed to every member of the community and associated with their fundamental rights, I might choose the term "legal citizenship." What I have in mind is something like the sense of citizenship invoked by T. H. Marshall in his famous book *Citizenship and Social Class*,[37] where he was concerned to tease out different strands of citizenship in a modern society. What I have been talking about in this lecture, we might associate with the specific dignity of what Marshall called "civil citizenship," though in his famous trichotomy of civil citizenship, political citizenship, and social citizenship, Marshall ran together under the "civil citizenship" heading ordinary civil liberties as well as rights of legal participation.

The civil element is composed of the rights necessary for individual freedom, liberty of the person, freedom of speech, thought and faith, the right to own property and to conclude valid contracts, and the right to justice. The last is of a different order from the others, because it is the right to defend and assert all one's rights on terms of equality with others and by due process of law. This shows us that the institutions most directly associated with civil rights are the courts of justice.[38]

I think that if I were undertaking the sort of disaggregation of layers of citizenship that T. H. Marshall undertook, I might perhaps want to distinguish between legal citizenship and civil citizenship (in the sense that associates the latter with the full enjoyment of civil liberty), though of course Marshall is right that the two usually go together. As well, Marshall traced not only the expansion of the citizenship idea into new areas—from civil to political to social—but also, in each area, the expansion of the benefits and rights of citizenship to all the human members of a society. And it is this phase, with regard to legal citizenship, that I am focusing on here.

Another term we might use is "equality before the law"—though that by itself does not convey the *height* of the legal status that we have universalized. And by some philosophers it is confused with formal equality—that is, impartial application of general norms according to their terms.[39] Formal equality may or may not be important, but it is not what I am talking about here. I am talking about the equal rights of self-application, hearing, and argument in relation to the legal process.

## 7. Representation

Obviously the sense in which we stand equal before the law is somewhat fictitious. But we should remember the suggestion in my first lecture, that dignity might be something constructed rather than natural. I think one of the main techniques we use to construct equal dignity in law is the artifice of legal representation. David

Luban has developed a persuasive account along these lines.[40] Luban asks: Why should litigants have lawyers? He cites as the basis of his answer the following principle: "[O]ne fails to respect [a person's] dignity...if on any serious matter one refuses even provisionally to treat his or her testimony about it as being in good faith." From this, Luban infers:

An immediate corollary to this principle is that litigants get to tell their stories and argue their understandings of the law. A procedural system that simply gagged a litigant and refused even to consider her version of the case would be, in effect, treating her story as if it did not exist, and treating her point of view as if it were literally beneath contempt. Once we accept that human dignity requires litigants to be heard, the justification of the advocate becomes clear. People may be poor public speakers. They may be inarticulate, unlettered, mentally disorganized, or just plain stupid. They may know nothing of the law, and so be unable to argue its interpretation....None of this should matter....Just as a non-English speaker must be provided an interpreter, the legally mute should have—in the very finest sense of the term—a mouthpiece. Thus, [the] argument connects the right to counsel with human dignity in two steps: first, that human dignity requires litigants to be heard, and second, that without a lawyer they cannot be heard.[41]

Forgive me for quoting Professor Luban at such length, but he makes exactly the point I want to make. We are committed to doing whatever it takes to secure the dignity of a hearing for everyone.

## 8. Coercion

Maybe the dignitarian account that I am giving makes law seem too "nice." Maybe I am obscuring the violent and coercive character of law.[42] Law kills people; it locks them up and throws away the key. And these are not aberrations; this is what law characteristically does. Where, it might be asked, is the dignity in that? Some have worried that "the entire enterprise, central to the criminal law, of regulating conduct through deterrence (that is, through the issuance of threats of deprivation and violence) is at odds with human dignity."[43] According to Lon Fuller, we have to choose between definitions of law that emphasize coercion and definitions of law that emphasize dignity.[44] I think this is a mistake. It is because law is coercive and its currency is life and death, freedom and incarceration, that its pervasive commitment to dignity is so momentous. Law is the exercise of power. But that power should be channeled through these processes, through forms and institutions like these, even when that makes its exercise more difficult or requires power occasionally to retire from the field defeated—this is exactly what is exciting about the equal dignity of legal citizenship in the context of the rule of law.

That is a wholesale answer to the objection. We might also give some retail responses. I have already mentioned the importance of self-application. Law looks wherever possible to voluntary compliance, which of course is not the same as saying we are never coerced, but which does leave room for the distinctively human trait of applying norms to one's own behavior. This is not a trick; it involves a genuinely respectful mode of coercion.

Max Weber is famous for observing that, although "the use of physical force is neither the sole, nor even the most usual, method of administration," still its threat "and in the case of need its actual use…is always the last resort when others have failed."[45] But it would be wrong to infer from this that law uses any means necessary to get its way. The use of torture, for example, is now banned by all legal systems.[46] Elsewhere I have argued that modern law observes this ban as emblematic of its commitment to a more general nonbrutality principle: "Law is not brutal in its operation;…it does not rule through abject fear and terror, or by breaking the will of those whom it confronts. If law is forceful or coercive, it gets its way by methods which respect rather than mutilate the dignity and agency of those who are its subjects."[47] I think this general aspiration is now fully internalized in our modern concept of law. The law

may force people to do things or go places they would not otherwise do or go to. But even when this happens, they are not herded
like cattle, broken like horses, beaten like dumb animals, or reduced
to a quivering mass of "bestial desperate terror."[48]

Finally: law punishes. But again—and increasingly this too is
internal to our conception of law—we deploy modes of punishment that do not destroy the dignity of those on whom it is being
administered. Some of this is the work of the specific dignitary
provisions we talked earlier, requiring that any punishment in-
flicted should be bearable—something that a person can endure,
without abandoning his or her elementary human functioning.[49]
One ought to be able to do one's time, take one's licks, while re-
maining upright and self-possessed. No one thinks the protection
of dignity is supposed to preclude *any* stigmatizing aspect of punishment. Whatever one's dignity, there is always something shameful in having to be dealt with on the basis that one has violated the
common standards set down in society for one's behavior. But an
aristocratic society might distinguish between the inevitable stigma
of the punishment accorded to a noble (in relation to his baseline
dignity) and the inevitable stigma of the punishment accorded to a
commoner or slave. There are punishments commensurate and
punishments incommensurate with one's status in both cases. I believe James Whitman is right in his suggestion that in some European countries, there has been a sort of leveling up—outlawing the
dehumanizing forms of punishment formerly visited upon low-
status persons: everyone who is punished is to be punished now as
though he were an errant noble rather than an errant slave.[50]

## 9. Dignity and Normativity

Is this account too naive? I know—we all know—that many political systems do not exhibit anything like the respect for dignity that
I have outlined here. Also, every country has to cope with the

burden of its own history, with vestiges of its commitment to an ideology of differential dignity. Think of the United States, for example, burdened by a history of slavery and institutionalized racism. When the Thirteenth Amendment abolished slavery, it did not do so unconditionally, but made an explicit exception for the treatment of prisoners—"Neither slavery nor involuntary servitude, except as a punishment for crime…, shall exist within the United States"—as though Americans were anxious to maintain at least a vestige of the sortal status implicated in the great denial of human dignity that had for years disfigured their Constitution. I do not need to tell you the impression that is created when one combines an understanding of this reservation with the staggering racial imbalances in American penitentiaries.

American defendants are sometimes kept silent and passive in American courtrooms by the use of technology that enables the judge to subject them to electric shocks if they misbehave.[51] Reports of prisoners being "herded" with cattle prods emerge from time to time.[52] Conditions in our prison are de facto terrorizing and well known to be so; even if they are not officially approved or authorized, we know that prosecutors feel free to make use of defendants' dread of this brutalization as a tactic in plea bargaining. And generally: we often participate in what Sanford Kadish once termed "the neglect of standards of decency and dignity that should apply whenever the law brings coercive measures to bear upon the individual."[53] Other examples and examples from other countries (France, the United Kingdom, Russia, Israel, etc.) could be multiplied. All have fallen short of the characterization given in this lecture.

A legal system is a normative order, both explicitly and implicitly. Explicitly it commits itself publicly to certain rules and standards. Some of these it actually upholds and enforces, but for others, in certain regards, it fails to do so. The explicit content of the norms recognized by the legal system provides us with a pretty straightforward basis for saying, on these occasions, that the legal system has fallen short of its own standards, without necessarily licensing the cynical conclusion that these were not its standards after all. This is because law is an institutionalized normative order, and there are ways of establishing the institutional existence (legal validity) of a given norm apart from its actually being fulfilled. A norm may be institutionalized in a given country inasmuch as it is proclaimed, posited, and published in that country, whether it is actually fulfilled or not. Or it may be, as we say, "honored in the breach," when its existence is revealed by the *way* in which we violate it (shamefacedly or furtively, for example).

Less straightforward is the case where a normative commitment is embodied *im*plicitly in the procedures and traditions of a system of governance. But I believe a similar logic obtains. The commitment to dignity that I think is evinced in our legal practices and institutions may be thought of as *immanently* present even though we sometimes fall short of it. Our practices sometimes convey a sort of promise and, as in moral life, it would be mistake to think that the only way to spot a real promise is to see what undertakings are actually carried out.[54] Law may credibly promise a respect for dignity, and yet betray that promise in various respects. Institutions can be imbued in their structures, practices, and procedures with the values and principles that they sometimes fall short of. In these cases, it is fatuous to present oneself as a simple cynic about their commitments or to neglect the power of imminent critique as the basis of a reproach for their shortcomings.

## 10. Back to Morality

At the beginning of these lectures, I said I would take my insights about dignity primarily from law. And I have combined this with an argument that the use of "*human* dignity" in constitutional and human rights law can be understood as the attribution of a high legal rank or status to every human being. I think we understand

now some of the ways in which legal systems constitute and vindicate human dignity, both in their explicit provisions and in their
overall modus operandi. Is it possible to say in an exactly analogous
sense that "morality" embodies a respect for human dignity?
I wonder. Morality (in the relevant sense of critical morality) is not
an *institutionalized* order; it is an array of reasons. And it may be
harder to think of morality as *proceduralized* in the way that legal
systems obviously are. On the other hand, moral thought does
sometimes use institutional metaphors to convey the character and
tendency of moral reasons: Kant's metaphor of the "kingdom of
ends" is the best-known example.[55] And though we think perhaps
less about moral due process than we ought to—we think about the
reactive attitudes, but not nearly enough about how accusation, ex-
planation, and response (including sanctions) ought to work in the
context of the pursuit of moral reproach—there are proceduralized
visions of morality in the work of philosophers like Jürgen Habermas and T. M. Scanlon, for example.[56]

Also we have to remember that a lot of what we call moral
thought is not devoted to the establishment of a moral order *analo-*
*gous* to a legal order, but is in fact oriented to the evaluation and
criticism of the legal order itself. Political morality is *about* law, and
so the place of dignity in political morality orients itself critically to
the place of dignity in the legal system. What I have been arguing
is that a lot of this moralizing involves *immanent critique*, rather
than bringing standards to bear that are independent of those the
law itself embodies. We evaluate law morally using (something
like) law's very own dignitarian resources.

What about the hypothesis I have pursued that *human* dignity
involves universalizing, rather than superseding, the connotations
of status, rank, and nobility that "dignity" traditionally conveyed?
These metaphors of transformation—of a change in the concept of
dignity—may not make sense when we talk about critical morality.[57] But we can certainly talk of changes in our *understanding* of
moral requirements. Moralists used to work with the notion that

there were different kinds of human being—low-status ones and high-status ones—and they have now dropped the idea of low-status human beings, assigning what was formerly high moral status to everyone.

Could respectable moral thought *ever* have differentiated in this way? Could morality have recognized different sortal statuses? Well we do this for the differences in moral considerability as between animals and humans. Or some do, and those who take this line claim that it is possible to draw it while still treating members of both classes morally. And there is no doubt that ideas about a distinctive dignity in which animals do not share play a large role in this distinction.[58] Could respectable moral thought ever have differentiated in this way *among humans*? Certainly it could; and it did. In 1907, the Clarendon Press at Oxford published the following in a two-volume treatise on moral philosophy by the Reverend Hastings Rashdall, concerning trade-offs between high culture and the amelioration of social and economic conditions:

It is becoming tolerably obvious at the present day that all improvement in the social condition of the higher races of mankind postulates the exclusion of competition with the lower races. That means that, sooner or later, the lower Well-being—it may be ultimately the very existence—of countless Chinamen or negroes must be sacrificed that a higher life may be possible for a much smaller number of white men.[59]

That is what passed for moral philosophy at Oxford a few generations ago. As far as I can tell there is nothing ironic in Rashdall's observation. It rests explicitly on what he calls "our comparative indifference to the welfare of the black races, when it collides with the higher Well-being of a much smaller European population."[60] For Rashdall, this is one of our considered judgments in what would now be described as *reflective equilibrium*: "Individuals, or races with higher capacities...have a right to more than merely equal consideration as compared to those of lower capacities."[61] This comes close to accepting a distinction among humans, analogous to that which we accept as between humans and animals.

We may not be able to make sense of the idea that *morality* (moral reasons) has changed in this regard; but *we* have certainly changed in our moral views (however deplorable our conduct continues to be). And again, I want to say that our moral views have moved *upward* in this respect, according to all men and women now the moral respect and consideration that Hastings Rashdall thought should be accorded to "a much smaller number of white men."

We might have moved in the opposite direction. Edmund Burke feared that we were. Deploring, in his *Reflections on the Revolution in France*, the violation of the serene and beauteous dignity of the queen of France, Burke lamented that

the age of chivalry is gone. That of sophisters, economists, and calculators, has succeeded.... Never, never more shall we behold that generous loyalty to rank and sex, that proud submission, that dignified obedience.... [N]ow all is to be changed.... All the decent drapery of life is to be rudely torn off. All the superadded ideas, furnished from the wardrobe of a moral imagination, which the heart owns, and the understanding ratifies, as necessary to cover the defects of our naked, shivering nature, and to raise it to dignity in our own estimation, are to be exploded as a ridiculous, absurd, and antiquated fashion. On this scheme of things, a king is but a man, a queen is but a woman; a woman is but an animal, and an animal not of the highest order.[62]

This is what reactionaries always say: if we abolish distinctions of rank, we will end up treating everyone like an animal, "and an animal not of the highest order." But the ethos of human dignity reminds us that there is an alternative: we can flatten out the scale of status and rank and leave Marie Antoinette more or less where she is. Everyone can eat cake or (more to the point) *everyone's* maltreatment—maltreatment of the lowliest criminal, abuse of the most despised of terror suspects—can be regarded as a sacrilege, a violation of human dignity, which (in the words of Edmund

Burke) ten thousand swords must leap from their scabbards to avenge.

## Notes

1. See, e.g., *The Earl of Lincoln against Roughton*, 79 Eng. Rep. 171; Cro. Jac. 196 (1606): "*Scandalum magnatum*; for that the defendant spake these words; 'My lord (innuendo the said Earl of Lincoln) is a base earl, and a paltry lord, and keepeth none but rogues and rascals like himself.' The defendant pleaded not guilty; and it was found against him. After verdict, it was moved in arrest of judgment, that these words were not actionable; for they touch him not in his life, nor in any matter of his loyalty, nor import him in any main point of his dignity, but are only words of spleen concerning his keeping of servants, which is not material. Yelverton and Fleming seemed to incline to that opinion; but Williams and Croke to the contrary, because they touched him in his honour and dignity; and to term him 'base lord' and 'paltry earl,' is matter to raise contempt betwixt him and the people, or the King's indignation against him: and such general words in case of nobility will maintain an action, although it will not in case of a common person."

2. I mean provisions like Article 7 of the ICCPR, "No one shall be subjected to torture or to cruel, inhuman, or degrading treatment or punishment," Article 3 of the ECHR, "No one shall be subjected to torture or to inhuman or degrading treatment or punishment," and Common Article 3 of the Geneva Conventions and Article 8 of the Rome Statute of the International Criminal Court, which prohibit "outrages upon personal dignity."

3. See, for example, Parts 3 and 3A of the United Kingdom's Public Order Act 1986.

4. See Heyman, *Free Speech and Human Dignity* and Jeremy Waldron, "Dignity and Defamation: The Visibility of Hate," *Harvard Law Review* 123 (2010): 1596.

5. ICCPR, Article 20 (2).

6. In *President of the Republic of South Africa and Another v. Hugo*, 1997 (4) SA (CC) 1, 1997 (6) BCLR 708, a case concerning gender discrimination, the South African Constitutional Court said that "the pur-

pose of [South Africa's] new constitutional and democratic order is the establishment of a society in which all human beings will be accorded equal dignity and respect regardless of their membership of particular groups" (ibid., at § 92). The court said this dignitarian conception lay at the heart of the prohibition of unfair discrimination.

7. *Minister of Finance v. Van Heerden*, 2004 (11) BCLR 1125, at § 116. See also the discussion in Waldron, "The Dignity of Groups."

8. *Law v. Canada (Minister of Employment and Immigration)* [1999] 1 S.C.R. § 51.

9. Ibid., §§ 53–54 and 72.

10. *R. v Kapp* [2008] SCR 41 at § 22: "Human dignity is an abstract and subjective notion that, even with the guidance of the four contextual factors, cannot only become confusing and difficult to apply; it has also proven to be an *additional* burden on equality claimants, rather than the philosophical enhancement it was intended to be."

11. R. James Fyfe, "Dignity as Theory: Competing Conceptions of Human Dignity at the Supreme Court of Canada," *Saskatchewan Law Review* 70 (2007): 1–26.

12. Alan Gewirth, "Rights and Virtues," *Review of Metaphysics* 38 (1985): 739–62, at p. 743.

13. See H. L. A. Hart, "Are There Any Natural Rights?" *Philosophical Review* 64 (1955): 175–91, reprinted in *Theories of Rights*, ed. Jeremy Waldron (Oxford: Oxford University Press, 1984): 77–90.

14. Ibid., p. 180 (*Theories of Rights*, p. 82).

15. But see H. L. A. Hart, "Bentham on Legal Rights," in *Oxford Essays in Jurisprudence*, 2nd series, ed. A. W. B. Simpson (Oxford: Clarendon Press, 1973): 171–201, for the beginnings of a retreat from this position.

16. Joel Feinberg, "The Nature and Value of Rights," *Journal of Value Inquiry* 4 (1970): 243–57.

17. Joel Feinberg, "Duties, Rights and Claims," *American Philosophical Quarterly* 3 (1966): 137–44, at p. 143.

18. Feinberg, "The Nature and Value of Rights," at p. 252.

19. Lon Fuller, *The Morality of Law* (New Haven: Yale University Press, 1964), esp. ch. 2.

20. See, e.g., H. L. A. Hart, "Book Review of Lon Fuller, *The Morality of Law*," *Harvard Law Review* 78 (1965): 1281–96, at p. 1284.

21. Fuller, *The Morality of Law*, p. 162.

22. See Henry M. Hart and Albert Sacks, *The Legal Process: Basic Problems in the Making and Application of Law*, ed. William N. Eskridge and Philip P. Frickey (Westbury, NY: Foundation Press, 1994), pp. 120–21.

23. It is part of the modern positivist understanding of law that we should appreciate the way in which norms are designed to *guide action* rather than simply coerce it. On the other hand, positivist jurisprudence is cautious about pursuing the implications that this may have for law's commitment to human dignity. Jules Coleman, for example, who places great emphasis on the way law guides action, is at pains to insist that the action-guiding function of law is not necessarily expressive of any dignitarian value. He tries to separate the issues in this way. In *The Practice of Principle: In Defence of a Pragmatist Approach to Legal Theory* (Oxford: Oxford University Press, 2001), pp. 194–95, Coleman writes: "Law just is the kind of thing that can realize some attractive ideals. That fact about law is not necessarily part of our concept of it."

24. Michael J. Meyer, "Dignity, Rights, and Self-Control," *Ethics* 99 (1989): 520–34.

25. Kant's moral psychology celebrated in individuals the power to subordinate impulse and desire to the lawlike demands of morality, revealing, as he says, "a life independent of animality." See Kant, *Critique of Practical Reason*, pp. 269–70 (5:162).

26. See Lon Fuller, "The Forms and Limits of Adjudication," *Harvard Law Review* 92 (1978): 353–409.

27. The legal philosopher who has done the most to develop this theme is Ronald Dworkin, particularly in *Law's Empire* (Cambridge: Harvard University Press, 1986).

28. See Arthur Chaskalson, "Human Dignity as a Constitutional Value," in Kretzmer and Klein, *The Concept of Human Dignity*: 133–44, at p. 140.

29. *Magna Carta* (1215), Article 21: "Earls and barons shall not be amerced except through their peers."

30. *Isabel, Countess of Rutland's Case*, 6 Co. Rep. 52 b, 77 Eng. Rep. 332 (1606), at p. 336.

31. Ibid., p. 333.

32. I take this phrase from Vlastos, "Justice and Equality," p. 55.

33. Graveson, *Status in the Common Law*, p. 2.

34. Is "status term" anything more than an abbreviation for all this detail? John Austin, *Lectures on Jurisprudence, or The Philosophy of Positive Law*, 5th edition, ed. Robert Campbell (London: John Murray, 1885), Lecture 40, pp. 687–88, did not think so. He believed that "[t]he sets of rights and duties, or of capacities and incapacities, inserted as *status* in the Law of Persons, are placed there merely for the sake of commodious exposition" and he treated each status term as "an ellipsis (or an abridged form of expression)" (ibid., p. 700). But Austin's skepticism neglects the idea, intimated in Graveson's definition, that a status attaches to a person when his occupying a certain position is a matter of social concern. Jeremy Bentham held a view of this kind. Austin (ibid., p. 699) noted that in *Traités de Législation*, Bentham defined a status as "un état domestique ou civil n'est qu'une base idéale, autour de laquelle se rangent des droits et des devoirs, et quelquefois des incapacités." The idea of the "base idéale"—the underlying reason—is crucial. The underlying reason explains how the various rights, duties, etc. hang together. Statuses package certain arrays of rights, duties, etc. under the auspices of a certain entrenched and ongoing concern in the law. No doubt Austin is right that status also has an exegetical use, in helping us organize and present legal knowledge in treatises, etc. But, as Bentham saw, its expository function is not just mnemonic, it is dynamic.

35. See *The 1928 Book of Common Prayer* (New York: Oxford University Press, 1993), p. 18: "O God, the Creator and Preserver of all mankind, we humbly beseech thee for all sorts and conditions of men; that thou wouldest be pleased to make thy ways known unto them, thy saving health unto all nations."

36. There might be different kinds of corporate personality. See Graveson, *Status in the Common Law*, pp. 72–78.

37. T. H. Marshall, *Citizenship and Social Class*, ed. Tom Bottomore (London: Pluto Press, 1992). See also Desmond King and Jeremy Waldron, "Citizenship, Social Citizenship and the Defence of Welfare Rights," *British Journal of Political Science* 18 (1988): 415–43, reprinted in Jeremy Waldron, *Liberal Rights: Collected Papers 1981–1991* (Cambridge: Cambridge University Press, 1993): 271–308.

38. Marshall, *Citizenship and Social Class*, p. 8.

39. See, e.g., Wojciech Sadurski, *Equality and Legitimacy* (New York: Oxford University Press, 2008), p. 94.

40. David Luban, *Legal Ethics and Human Dignity* (Cambridge: Cambridge University Press, 2007) and David Luban, "Lawyers as Upholders of Human Dignity (When They Aren't Busy Assaulting It)," *University of Illinois Law Review* 2005: 815–45.

41. Luban, "Lawyers as Upholders of Human Dignity," p. 819.

42. See, e.g. Austin Sarat and Thomas Kearns, "A Journey through Forgetting: Toward a Jurisprudence of Violence," in *The Fate of Law*, ed. Austin Sarat and Thomas Kearns (Ann Arbor: University of Michigan Press, 1991): 209–74.

43. See Meir Dan-Cohen, "Decision Rules and Conduct Rules: On Acoustic Separation in Criminal Law," *Harvard Law Review* 97 (1984): 625–77 at pp. 672–73.

44. Fuller, *The Morality of Law*, p. 108.

45. Max Weber, *Economy and Society*, ed. Guenther Roth and Claus Wittich (Berkeley: University of California Press, 1978), p. 54.

46. This is why the recent proposals in the United States to introduce judicial torture warrants and to make torture a procedure in law (not just in Blackstone's words—Morrison, *Blackstone's Commentaries on the Laws of England*, 4:257 [ch. 25]—"an engine of state") aroused such anger in parts of the legal community. The proposal is mooted and discussed in Alan Dershowitz, *Why Terrorism Works: Understanding the Threat, Responding to the Challenge* (New Haven: Yale University Press, 2002), pp. 156–63. See generally, Jeremy Waldron, "Torture and Positive Law," *Columbia Law Review* 105 (2005): 1681–1750 (reprinted in Waldron, *Torture, Terror and Trade-Offs*, pp. 186–260), at pp. 1718–20 (*Torture, Terror, and Trade-Offs*, pp. 247–52), for a fuller discussion.

47. This is adapted from Waldron, "Torture and Positive Law," at p. 1726 (*Torture, Terror, and Trade-Offs*, p. 232).

48. Hannah Arendt, *The Origins of Totalitarianism*, new edition (New York: Harcourt Brace Jovanovich, 1973), p. 441.

49. See Waldron, *Torture, Terror, and Trade-Offs*, p. 307.

50. See Whitman, "Human Dignity in Europe and the United States."

51. See, e.g., Harriet Chiang, "Justices Limit Stun Belts in Court," *San Francisco Chronicle*, August 23, 2002, p. A7 and William Glaberson,

"Electric Restraint's Use Stirs Charges of Cruelty to Inmates," *New York Times,* June 8, 1999, p. A1.

52. See, e.g., "37 Prisoners Sent to Texas Sue Missouri," *St. Louis Post-Dispatch* (Missouri), September 18, 1997, p. 3B: "Missouri prisoners alleging abuse in a jail in Texas have sued their home state and officials responsible for running the jail where a videotape showed inmates apparently being beaten and shocked with stun guns," and Mike Bucsko and Robert Dvorchak, "Lawsuits Describe Racist Prison Rife with Brutality," *Pittsburgh Post-Gazette,* April 26, 1998, p. B1.

53. Sanford H. Kadish, "Francis A. Allen: An Appreciation," *Michigan Law Review* 85 (1986): 401–5, at p. 403.

54. Cf. Jeremy Waldron, "Does Law Promise Justice?" *Georgia State University Law Review* 17 (2001): 759–88, at pp. 760–61. For analogous arguments about justice, see Philip Selznick, *The Moral Commonwealth: Social Theory and the Promise of Community* (Berkeley: University of California Press, 1992), p. 443: "Law is not necessarily just, but it does promise justice." See also John Gardner, "The Virtue of Justice and the Character of Law," *Current Legal Problems* 53 (2000): 31–52.

55. Kant, *Groundwork,* pp. 83–88 (4:433–34).

56. See Jürgen Habermas, *Moral Consciousness and Communicative Action* (Cambridge: MIT Press, 1991) and T. M. Scanlon, *What We Owe to Each Other* (Cambridge: Harvard University Press, 1998).

57. John Finnis once observed, in *Natural Law and Natural Rights* (Oxford: Clarendon Press, 1980), p. 24, that "of natural law itself there could, strictly speaking, be no history," meaning that natural law is a timeless set of values, reasons, and requirements.

58. Psalm 8:4–8, for example: "What is man, that thou art mindful of him?…For thou hast made him a little lower than the angels, and hast crowned him with glory and honour. Thou madest him to have dominion over the works of thy hands; thou hast put all things under his feet: all sheep and oxen, yea, and the beasts of the field; the fowl of the air, and the fish of the sea, and whatsoever passeth through the paths of the seas."

59. Hastings Rashdall, *The Theory of Good and Evil: A Treatise on Moral Philosophy,* 2nd edition (Oxford University Press, 1924), 1:237–38. Rashdall appends a footnote: "The exclusion is far more difficult to justify in the case of people like the Japanese, who are equally civilized but have fewer wants than the Western" (ibid., p. 238). The author continued: "If

we do defend it" (and he had no doubt that we would), "we distinctly adopt the principle that higher life is intrinsically, in and for itself, more valuable than lower life, though it may only be attainable by fewer persons, and may not contribute to the greater good of those who do not share it."

60. Ibid., p. 241.

61. Ibid., p. 242.

62. Edmund Burke, *Reflections on the Revolution in France*, ed. Leslie Mitchell (Oxford: Oxford University Press, 1993), p. 77.

# Comments

# Dignity Past and Present

## Michael Rosen

## 1.

I am very much in sympathy with Jeremy Waldron's basic project but I also have some disagreements both about analytical matters and historical ones. I shall start by retracing some of the steps that Waldron took in his lectures and enlarging on what he said at some points. I am not sure whether he will find all of what I have to say congenial to his project, but my points are offered in an admiring and, I hope, constructive spirit.

Let me start by emphasizing my agreement with Waldron, because, although I shall spend longer on the points where we diverge, my agreement with him is, I think, more fundamental. Waldron presents his views about the nature of dignity in the context of a wider conception of the history of equality that we can call an "expanding circle" view, or, as we could also say (and I think that Waldron will not see this label as the slur that it might be to some) a "Whig" view. Put simply, this is the thought that a political (and social and legal) conception that was originally applied to a relatively narrow class of beings has come to be extended over time until it is, to all intents and purposes, universal. There are those who would quarrel with this picture both historically and philosophically—because it casts a complacently meliorist glow over many historical crimes and horrors and because, they believe, to universalize originally contrastive value-language is to cover over its oppositional character. To the first objection, I can say nothing except that I think that one can accept the historical facts without having to see them in the perspective of a providentialist teleology. The philosophical objection can, of course, be formulated in different ways, in the language of Derridean deconstruction or of Carl Schmitt, according to taste, but the basic thought was well enough expressed by W. S. Gilbert's Grand Inquisitor in *The Gondoliers*: "When everybody's somebody / nobody's anybody." Against that, Waldron sides with the gondoliers:

> The Aristocrat who banks with Coutts—
> The Aristocrat who hunts and shoots—
> The Aristocrat who cleans our boots—
> They all shall equal be!

> The Noble Lord who rules the state—
> The Noble Lord who cleans the plate—
> The Noble Lord who scrubs the grate—
> They all shall equal be!

I am with Waldron. I see nothing incoherent in the idea that we should all be of high rank, however that came about. If you think that there is *nothing more* to that status than the differentiation of superior and inferior—if, like e.e. cummings, you think that freedom is "some under's mere above"—then the exercise will seem absurd and fruitless. But it seems only right to recognize that, if we are all Aristocrats and Noble Lords (and Ladies!) then it is an open question what elements of aristocratic status behavior we carry with us. The story that Waldron tells is principally one of "leveling up"—that we should all be accorded the treatment previously reserved for those with the highest status—and this is, I think, generally true. But it is not always so. There can be "leveling down" too—an aristocrat would once have addressed his servants by their first names but expected to be addressed by title himself. Now employer and employee expect to be on first-name terms.

I am also intrigued, if not exactly convinced, by Waldron's idea that we can understand important moral conceptions by moving, if I can put it this way, from politics to metaphysics. In contrast to

what might seem to be a commonsense view of the enterprise of
moral theory—that we should first discover what are fundamental
moral values and then look to legal and political forms within which
they may be realized—we may do better, he thinks, to see those
values as themselves *products* of social (that is, legal and political)
institutions. This may sound like *conventionalism* (I was going to
say "mere conventionalism")—the idea that there is nothing more
to the concept of human equality, for example, than the fact that we
have decided to treat one another as equals. In which case, you may
ask, who are *we* to decide? And why should our choice have any
normative force? I do not believe that this is quite what Waldron
means, but his view does, I think, have a "bootstrapping" quality
that some may find off-putting. His position, to my mind, has more
in common with Rawlsian moral constructivism than with conventionalism, but I shall say no more about these important issues of
methodological principle because I have issues more specific to the
idea of dignity to discuss.

## 2.

And now I come to my disagreements. I have reservations about
what Waldron has to say that are strategic, historical, conceptual,
and (I say this with all diffidence as a nonlawyer) legal. These different aspects are connected. In short, I am skeptical about his strat-
egy of using reflection on the law to resolve moral disagreement
because I think that there is a lot more conflict (and downright confusion) about dignity in its use in the law than he allows. Moreover,
I think that such disagreement and lack of clarity is by no means
accidental. On the contrary, it seems to me that the agreement on
dignity that coincided with the conclusion of the most fundamental
modern legal and human rights documents in which "dignity"
plays a prominent role—I am thinking above all of the Universal
Declaration of Human Rights and the Basic Law of the German

Federal Republic—was the product of a very particular confluence of ideas (and a willingness to make political compromises) on the part of different groups and interests at an unusual, exceptionally important, point in history. In my view, that time has gone. It is not that the agreement that it contained has been abrogated but rather that its scope has been revealed to be insufficient to cover the disagreement that was already latent. That disagreement about dignity has reemerged is because the concept has an independent background that is more complex and antagonistic than Waldron recognizes. I shall develop this argument (and offer my more constructive thoughts) later in this contribution. To start with, I should like to say something about Waldron's approach to the concept and his account of its history.

Waldron canvasses two alternative approaches—one by which we advance from philosophy to the law, in the other from law to philosophy. In the first case, he explains, "we look for the sense that moral philosophers have made of [dignity]" and then "we look to see how adequately or how clumsily that moral idea has been represented in the work of the drafters of statutes or constitutions, and human rights conventions or in the decisions that constitute our legal doctrines and precedents." Waldron, however, endorses the opposite approach. Dignity, he asserts, has its "natural habitat" in the law. It is a "constructive idea with a foundational and explicative function," like "utility." It has been imported by philosophers in order to make sense of ordinary moral ideas, although it is, he claims (on the authority of a lunchtime conversation with Joseph Raz) "not a term that crops up much in ordinary moral conversation." So dignity, even if we acknowledge it as the ground of rights, "need not be treated in the first instance as a moral idea"; it should, rather, be seen as a "juridical" one.

I have to say that I disagree with everything that has just been said. It proceeds, first of all, from what is, in my view, a false alternative: either we move from moral philosophy to law or from

law to moral philosophy. But why should we not move back-
wards and forwards between the two; why give one or the other
priority? And why not acknowledge the law as one of the forms
(a particular form, of course) of moral discourse? Waldron's view
is that there is a class of concepts that he calls "juridical" that are
endogenous to the law, even though they may at the same time
provide law with its grounding doctrines. "Law," he says, "envelops...and constitutes these ideas; it does not just borrow them
from morality." This is an intriguing and ambitious claim. I must
say that I doubt that there are such purely legal foundational
ideas, but, if there are, then, as I hope to show, dignity is not one.
(Which is not to say, I should emphasize, that it is "just bor-
rowed" from morality—the fact that "dignity" has extralegal
origins does not entail that it is not transformed by being placed
in a legal context.)

The assertion that dignity does not crop up much in "ordinary
moral conversation" seems to me so obviously wrong that I can't
see how anyone except a distinguished moral philosopher whose
"ordinary moral conversation" takes place in an atmosphere of so-
phisticated analytical reflection could reasonably think so. I have no
time to give extensive evidence, so I shall just give an example from
recent experience. Just after receiving the draft of Waldron's lectures I was talking with a friend in the UK who has the misfortune
to be receiving treatment at the country's leading cancer hospital.
As she arrived for her treatment, she told me, she could hardly get
into the building for a crowd of press photographers scrambling
and fighting for a shot of a well-known tabloid celebrity, then in the
terminal stages of cancer. My friend (who is not a lawyer and has
never, to my knowledge, opened a philosophy book) shouted at
them "For God's sake! Give her some dignity!" "Dignity" appears
in ordinary moral conversation all the time, it seems to me. If anything, it is moral philosophers in the academy—Anglo-American
ones at least (the situation is somewhat different in Germany)—
who have given it little attention.

If I understand Waldron's argument rightly, the best evidence that dignity is an autonomous legal concept—a "juridical" one, in his sense—is that it is legal in origin. It is, he says, "a matter of status" and "status is a legal conception." Hence "we should look first at the bodies of law that relate status to rank (and to right and privilege) and see what if anything is retained of these ancient conceptions." If we are to follow him, dignity is a tolerably well-defined juridical concept that is suitable to play a foundational role (or, as he charmingly puts it, "foundation-ish" role—he doesn't go the whole hog) for human rights discourse.

I, on the other hand, see a concept whose history reveals deep conceptual ambiguities and tensions, tensions that require clarification. As it seems to me, the agreement that came about at the end of the Second World War represented a moment of precarious though precious compromise—but it is an agreement that has subsequently, unsurprisingly, fallen apart as the compromise proved incapable of playing the foundational role hoped for. But I shall leave these reflections for later. For now, I should like to sketch an account of the concept of dignity that is rather different than Waldron's.

## 3.

Although I shall not trace the origins of dignity in all its details, it seems to me indisputable that the main classical source is Cicero. He writes in the *De Officiis*, for example: "But in every investigation into the nature of duty, it is vitally necessary for us to remember always how vastly superior is man's nature to that of cattle and other animals: their only thought is for bodily satisfactions.... Man's mind, on the contrary, is developed by study and reflection.... From this we may learn that sensual pleasure is wholly unworthy of the dignity of the human race."[1] The phrase *cum dignitate otium* (dignity with leisure) is used by him to characterize the condition of the *optimates* in a well-ordered republic.[2] Certainly, dignity here is a status term in a general sense, although not, I think, a juridical one. But it is to Cicero too that we can trace another seminal sense of dignity: the contrast between "grace" and "dignity" as rhetorical modes—the light and sparkling against the weighty and sonorous. The distinction is a permanent feature of the rhetorical and critical literature all the way to Lord Kames's *Elements of Criticism* (1762). This rhetorical context, although limitations of time mean that I shall have little to say about it, should not be forgotten, for it inflects the way in which the idea of dignity has been given content— the way in which users of the term have connected the idea of dignity with an understanding of what it is to be *dignified*.

Let me leap now to the early modern world and come to earth with Francis Bacon who, conveniently for me, short of space as I am, uses "dignity" in more than one language and with more than one sense. Thus (in 1623) Bacon published an expanded translation into Latin of his *Advancement of Learning* under the title *De dignitate et augmentis scientarum*. I suggest that the most immediately natural translation for *dignitate* here is "worth" or "value" (I will argue in support of this later). Note that "dignity" is being applied to an abstract entity—learning—so it cannot be in any legal sense of the term a status concept. Here, on the other hand, is a quotation from Bacon's Essay "Of Great Place." "The rising into place is laborious, and by pains men come to greater pains; and it is sometimes base, and by indignities men come to dignities."[3] So here we also have an opposition of high and low status, as well as a description of the behavior associated with such status of just the sort that Waldron calls our attention to. These different senses are evidently coexistent.

The use of "dignity" as an evaluative term of general application rather than as a status term of a social or legal character applied to human beings is widespread by this time. Milton in the preface to his 1644 essay "Of the Doctrine and Discipline of Divorce" argues that the value of marriage lies in the character of the social relationship between men and women. Thus he writes, "God in the first ordaining of marriage, taught us to what end he did it, in words expressly implying that the apt and cheerful conversation of man with woman, to comfort and refresh him against the evil of solitary life, not mentioning the purpose of generation till afterwards, as being but *a secondary end in dignity, though not in necessity*"[4] (my emphasis). Is this use of dignity to characterize the nature of the value that something has deeply rooted or merely idiosyncratic? I think it is clearly the former. Indeed, the most seminal of Catholic thinkers, St. Thomas Aquinas, gives us an explicit definition of dignity in his *Commentary on the Sentences* that says just that: "Dignity signifies something's goodness on account of itself."[5] In other words, "dignity" is a term for, as we would now put it, something's intrinsic value—the value that it has by occupying its appropriate place within God's creation, as revealed by Scripture and by natural law.

I am convinced that this sense of dignity as the intrinsic value of something permeates dignity discourse, particularly Catholic. So Pico della Mirandola's now-famous oration (which only received its title *De dignitate hominis* quite some years after Pico's death) asks the question of what the proper place and value of human beings is within God's creation, *De dignitate et augmentis scientarum* the place and value of learning, and so on. In 1659, for example, Bishop Bossuet, no less, preached a sermon "Sur l'eminente dignité des pauvres dans l'Église." Bossuet, you may recall, was court preacher at the court of Louis XIV and (to put it mildly) no friend to social equality. His attribution of "eminent dignity" to the poor is not to give them equal (or even higher) status with the nobility but to assert their value within a properly ordered hierarchy. The distinction between this and the status conception of dignity presented by Waldron may seem subtle, but it is indispensable if we are to understand the Catholic view of dignity.

To show this let me jump again over a couple of centuries to Pope Leo XIII. Leo XIII is no doubt best known today for the encyclical

*Rerum Novarum* of 1891, dealing with the relationship between Labor and Capital, that established the idea of the "dignity of labor" within the Catholic tradition. We would be quite wrong to think that Leo defends the dignity of labor in terms of a conception of status equality. Here, for example, is an extract from Leo's encyclical *Quod Apostolici Muneris* of 1878:

> For, He who created and governs all things has, in His wise providence, appointed that the things which are lowest should attain their ends by those which are intermediate, and these again by the highest. Thus, as even in the kingdom of heaven He hath willed that the choirs of angels be distinct and some subject to others, and also in the Church has instituted various orders and a diversity of offices, so that all are not apostles or doctors or pastors, so also has He appointed that there should be various orders in civil society, differing in dignity, rights, and power, whereby the State, like the Church, should be one body, consisting of many members, some nobler than others, but all necessary to each other and solicitous for the common good. (6)[6]

Leo is not simply concerned to assert the propriety of a hierarchically ordered society. In *Arcanum divinae sapientiae* (1880), he asserts the inequality of men and women in marriage:

> The woman, because she is flesh of his flesh and bone of his bone, must be subject to her husband and obey him; [an invalid inference from a false premise, if ever I saw one!] not, indeed, as a servant, but as a companion, so that her obedience shall be wanting in neither honour nor dignity. (11)

Note that "dignity" here is not an attribute of the person in question—the wife—but is applied to an aspect of a social relationship in which she finds herself, "her obedience." The ascription of "dignity" is not being used to raise the status of a subordinate being but to ascribe value to subordination itself. This corresponds to something fundamental about the way in which "dignity" has been used in the Catholic tradition (it may also explain, incidentally, why so many egalitarians I know who have had a Catholic education are allergic to the concept of dignity).

## 4.

But why have I belabored this point and skipped over the egalitarian dimension of dignity whose development we owe to some complex combination of Kant's moral philosophy, Schiller's moralized aesthetics, and the abolition of status hierarchies associated with the French Revolution? It is not by any means to deny or belittle the development that Waldron has very ably depicted. My point rather—the point of this contribution—is to argue that we need to understand the Catholic conception of dignity to appreciate the very special character of what took place when the fundamental documents for the use of dignity in modern legal-political discourse—that is, in my view, the Universal Declaration of Human Rights (1948) and the *Grundgesetz* (Basic Law) of the German Federal Republic (1949)—were agreed. In both cases, we have an understanding of dignity that merits the label "overlapping consensus." Dignity takes a primary place in both documents—in the first article of each. More significantly, dignity is closely associated with a universal conception of human rights. This is obvious in the Universal Declaration, which starts with the words "All human beings are born free and equal *in dignity and rights*" and only slightly less so in the *Grundgesetz* in which the second clause of the first article states that "The German people therefore [that is, in virtue of the inviolable dignity of human beings] commits itself to inviolable and inalienable human rights as the basis of every human society" (Art. 1, 2). To those who read these documents with eyes informed by post-1789 egalitarianism, the connection between dignity and rights may seem evident and trivial. Looking back at the antiegalitarianism with which the concept of dignity is associated in the Catholic tradition, however, shows that it should not be taken for granted. Indeed, the contrast between dignity and rights is still alive. Take the Cairo Declaration on Human Rights in Islam (1990 by the Organization of the Islamic Conference) whose Article 6, in contrast to the Universal Declaration, asserts that women have "equal dignity" but, conspicuously, not equal rights.

Both the Universal Declaration and the *Grundgesetz* were adopted with the support of the Catholic Church, which participated actively in the drafting process in each case. The result was a clear endorsement on the part of the Church of a Christian commitment to a democratic, rights-respecting polity and to a social order based on a fundamental equality of status. It represented nothing less, I think, than the Church's final peace treaty (after a mere 160 years) with the principles of the French Revolution. For expanding-circle Whiggish egalitarians like Waldron and myself this is a development to be welcomed with open-hearted joy. Indeed, for those of us whose egalitarianism has a touch of sociological Hegelianism, it is a fact of prime importance for the understanding of international political society in the last sixty years.

Nevertheless, this did not represent the acceptance by Catholicism of the status-based conception of equality that Waldron endorses, so much as a confluence of different traditions. If I am not so sanguine as Waldron about the concept of dignity, it is not because I think that the Catholic commitment to a conception of human dignity that entails political and social equality is anything other than robust, avowed differences regarding its philosophical foundations notwithstanding. Although a few diehards may still fight on, I think that there is not the slightest chance that the Church will go back to its antiegalitarian past. Nevertheless, foundational differences lead to disagreement regarding both the scope and the content of the idea of dignity—differences that make themselves apparent in the use of "dignity" both within and outside the law.

I have argued that Waldron's picture of dignity as "a term used to indicate a high-ranking legal, political, and social status," and of "*human* dignity" as "the assignment of such a high-ranking status to everyone" is oversimplified. It ignores, I claimed, a very important

strand of thought proceeding from Aquinas's idea that "Dignity signifies something's goodness on account of itself [*propter seipsum*]"[7] To the extent that this conception has dignity as a status concept it is only that everything that has intrinsic value does so in virtue of occupying its proper place in a divine order. Dignity in this sense can be found in all parts of God's creation—in human beings, certainly, but also in abstract objects (such as "learning") and human relations (such as marriage or obedience). From this perspective, the question of human dignity is an open question—it invites an account of the proper place of human beings in the world and what their essential, valuable characteristics are. The answer that all share in a high rank just in virtue of being human is one, but only one, such account.

I emphasized this point to indicate how remarkable an achievement it was to bring together the theological conception of dignity with the liberal conception of equal human rights in the founding documents of modern dignity-based law and politics—the Universal Declaration and the German *Grundgesetz*. I now want to argue that the tensions in the notion of dignity are deep and fundamental, both conceptually and sociopolitically. The picture that Waldron gives of an emerging egalitarian consensus is too optimistic because its scope is, at best, narrow. However, I also want to use these conceptual and historical reflections positively, to propose a constructive suggestion about the proper use of the notion of dignity that, although it differs markedly from Waldron's, is, I hope, complementary to his and in its spirit.

## 5.

Why is the placement of "human dignity" at the outset of both Universal Declaration and *Grundgesetz* so important? For Waldron the mere presence of the phrase "human dignity" entails the acceptance that all human beings share a "high-ranking legal, political, and moral status." If I am right, though, the acceptance of a common "human dignity" leaves it open whether they share legal, political, and social equality—the Catholic tradition, at least until recently, saw no incompatibility between human dignity and a strongly hierarchical view of human society. It was no accident, surely, that the notion of human dignity was embedded in the prewar constitutions of countries such as Portugal and Spain—no paradises of democracy and equal rights! What is crucial, then, about the Universal Declaration and the *Grundgesetz* is the close connection between human dignity and equal human rights. Does that mean that the idea of dignity falls away—like the wrapping on the Easter egg—and that it is to the rights themselves that we must look for substance? Not necessarily, for it might be that the idea of dignity could be connected to our conception of human rights, whether by giving them a foundation or by fixing their content—or perhaps (best of all!) fixing their content by giving them a foundation. Waldron, of course, has given us a distinctive account of how this might work. Dignity, he argues, is a legal conception that requires no extralegal (that is, moral or metaphysical) foundation, but that can itself play a foundational role (or, as he says, "foundation-ish") for human rights. I shall return to Waldron's account below but, for the moment, I want to draw attention to two quite different moral conceptions, both of which, I claim, are at work in modern dignity and rights discourse. Not only do they offer quite different foundations for the concept of dignity—that may be no very bad thing if the effect is that of an overlapping consensus—but they also give quite different answers to the question of who (or what) has dignity and what content (in the form of rights?) the possession of dignity entails. The first conception can be found expressed with characteristic economy and precision by James Griffin:

Autonomy is a major part of rational agency, and rational agency constitutes what moral philosophers have often called, with unnecessary obscurity, the dignity of the person.[8]

A similar view—if more polemically and less subtly expressed—has been advanced by Ruth Macklin. Dignity, she claims, "means no more than respect for persons or their autonomy."[9] Who are "rational agents"? What does it mean to say that they are "autonomous"? And how is that autonomy to be "respected"? Of course, the answers to those questions are various and complicated, but for my purposes here it is not necessary to pursue them in detail. What is important is the connection that is made between dignity and rational agency, on the one hand, and (via autonomy) choice on the other. On this view, it is rational agents who are the central (if not the only) beneficiaries of dignity and it is their power of choice that requires respect.

Does this conception of dignity play a central role in modern dignity discourse? Yes indeed! Consider the celebrated "Philosophers' Brief" on assisted suicide.[10] The six philosophers (Dworkin, Nagel, Nozick, Rawls, Scanlon, and Thomson) argued that the patient-plaintiffs in the case before the Supreme Court had what they termed a "constitutionally protected liberty interest" in hastening their own deaths. Such a "constitutionally protected liberty interest" could be inferred, they argued, from the Court's own jurisprudence. Significantly, they quoted the Supreme Court's decision in *Planned Parenthood v. Casey* (505 U.S. 833, 851 (1992)) in which the Court referred to "the right of people to make their own decisions about matters involving the most intimate and personal choices a person may make in a lifetime, choices central to personal dignity and autonomy." Dignity, then, requires individuals to be allowed the power of choice over matters that they consider to be of the highest importance to themselves.

Not surprisingly, the voluntarism associated with the autonomy conception of human dignity is forcefully rejected by the Catholic

Church (as well as by many other religious groups), for example by Pope John Paul II in his encyclicals *Veritatis Splendor* (1993) and *Evangelium Vitae* (1995). In *Veritatis Splendor* the pope recognizes that "[the] heightened sense of the dignity of the human person…certainly represents one of the positive achievements of modern culture" (31). On the other hand, it is characteristic of atheism and "doctrines which have lost the sense of the transcendent" that they should "exalt freedom to such an extent that it becomes an absolute, which would then be the source of values" (32). In *Evangelium Vitae,* John Paul II identifies a "remarkable contradiction" between "the various declarations of human rights" that acknowledge "the value and dignity of every individual as a human being" and what he sees as the repudiation of those rights in practice (18, 19). The problem, in the pope's view, is a voluntarist conception of human dignity, "the mentality which carries the concept of subjectivity to an extreme and even distorts it, and recognizes as a subject of rights only the person who enjoys full or at least incipient autonomy" (19).

There, you might think, we have the problem in its starkest form. Certainly, the liberal-humanistic and the theistic conceptions of human dignity (at least in the latter's modern, Catholic form) have come to agree on a very great deal in accepting certain central social and political rights for adult human beings—the rights associated with democratic self-government and basic social equality—but, when it comes to questions of medical and biological ethics—issues such as abortion, suicide, sexual morality, medical experimentation, and genetic engineering—there is simply no common ground. On the one side, valuable beings are seen as rational agents and what is to be protected is, fundamentally, their autonomous agency; on the other, we have the denial that human choice can ever override the intrinsic and inviolable value that attaches to all "human life."

Here is where Waldron—brave man!—enters the fray. His idea is that we should not look for a foundational concept to act as a basis for human dignity but that it should be understood as "a high-ranking legal, political, and social status" that is assigned to "everyone." Will this bold proposal bring peace to the battlefield of (moral) metaphysics? I fear not. First of all and most obviously, who is "everyone"? Does it include zygotes, embryos, fetuses, the severely mentally handicapped, and those in persistent vegetative states? If there was an answer to this question in Waldron's lectures I have missed it. Moreover, what substantive consequences follow from extending the idea of high status to all human beings? Many of the forms of social interaction characteristic of high status when the latter was part of a hierarchical society were forms of deference and submission. Waldron has given us several vivid and (to me) persuasive examples of ways in which the law may be used to defend the "high rank or dignity of the ordinary person" by protecting her from degradation, insult, and contempt. (Waldron mentions as a separate category the use of dignity in order to protect against invidious discrimination. To my understanding, in those jurisdictions within which dignity has been invoked to distinguish benign from invidious discrimination, it is the contempt and insult implicit in discrimination that is held to constitute the dignitary harm, so I don't see this as a separate case.)

## 6.

What these cases show, however, in my opinion, is somewhat different from what Waldron has in mind. They turn, it seems to me, on the notion of *respect*. To make my point, let me start with a little piece of analysis. We are agreed that human dignity is to be respected. But what does that amount to? If I respect the speed limit, I do so by driving below a certain speed. If I respect your right to free speech, I do so by not placing any impediment on your speaking. In general, I respect the law by keeping to it and I respect rights by not infringing them. Let me call this "respect-as-observance." Is that what is involved in respecting human dignity? If so, we need to know the content of dignity; without it we could not respect dignity any more than we could observe the law without knowing what it was. Does dignity entail something distinct from the "inviolable and inalienable human rights" that the *Grundgesetz* says follow from human dignity (in which case, what might that be?) or is it simply a way of saying that human beings are entitled to this package of rights, whatever they are? But Waldron (I don't know how deliberately) is, it seems clear to me, invoking a different kind of respect. In protecting the individual from degradation, insult, and contempt we are requiring that people act towards her in ways that are substantively respectful. To respect their dignity in this sense means to treat them *with respect*. Let me call this "respect-as-respectfulness."

If I am right, this is a very important point indeed. On the one hand, it gives content to the idea of human dignity—gives an answer to those who allege that there is nothing more to the idea of "dignity" than rhetorical wrapping paper for a set of substantive rights-claims. On the other, it implies that dignitary harms are harms of a special kind. What degradation, insult, and contempt have in common is that they are expressive or symbolic harms, ones in which the elevated status of human beings *fails to be acknowledged*. I agree with this understanding of dignitary harm very much but note that this understanding of dignity as requiring "respect-as-respectfulness" has a very important consequence. If we take the view that dignitary harms are essentially symbolic—failures to express respect for status—then we must believe *either* that all violations of fundamental human rights are essentially symbolic *or* that dignity cannot fulfill the role assigned to it in our basic human rights documents—to provide a foundation for the rights embodied in them.

For my part, I embrace the second option. It seems to me evident that not all violations of rights are symbolic harms. When you torture me, you do indeed humiliate and degrade me, but the harm is not just that: you cause me extreme pain and thereby deprive me of effective self-control. To do so would be impermissible and would violate a human right whether or not it was associated with expressions of contempt. (A moral position exists by which *every* wrong consists in acting in ways that fail to express respect—according to which the wrong I do you when I punch you on the nose does not consist in the pain that I cause you so much as the lack of respect it shows for your personhood. But here is not the place for a discussion of Kantian ethics, fascinating and pertinent as it might be.)

Thus there is, I think, a distinct class of dignitary harms of a symbolic or expressive character and it is here that the value of dignity may properly be connected with the wider, aesthetic idea of the *dignified*. Respecting someone's dignity involves treating them "with dignity." What that amounts to varies, naturally, between cultures and contexts, but there are some striking common themes. One, on which Waldron has concentrated, is that when there are (or were) marked demarcations of social status between human beings, to treat someone with dignity is to treat them in a way that expressively attributes to them the highest status. Another characteristic demarcation, however (which goes back to Cicero's *De Officiis*) is that human dignity is expressed by behavior that marks the distinction between human beings and animals—for example, in upright gait, through the wearing of clothes, in eating subject to a code of table manners, defecating (and copulating) in private, and, finally, by disposing of human remains according to prescribed rituals. The precise content of such rituals varies widely—should corpses be buried, burned, or left to be eaten by vultures?—but their existence and, as it seems, symbolic force, is strikingly general. To compel human beings to violate such symbolic codes is to subject them to gross indignity.

But if I am right in thinking that this is what is distinctive about dignitary harm, then, shocking though it may be (remember the shameful pictures from Abu Ghraib prison), it leaves a possible doubt about its fundamental importance. Not that symbolic harms are not real harms—but they cannot, surely, be the most fundamental. After all, the worst of what the Nazi state did to the Jews was not the humiliation of herding them into cattle trucks and forcing them to live in conditions of unimaginable squalor; it was to murder them.

If, like me, you feel the force of this, I offer in conclusion a thought that has been extensively supported by Jonathan Glover in his wonderful book *Humanity: A Moral History of the Twentieth Century*.[11] One of the features that have characterized many of the most violent and destructive acts of the twentieth century has been the humiliation and symbolic degradation of the victims. We can find examples in the Nazi concentration camp, the Soviet gulag, Cambodia, or the Balkans. It seems to be a fact about human nature that human beings are able more easily to engage in the most violent behavior towards one another if at the same time they can expressively deny the humanity of their victims. If this is so then the preservation of our fellow human beings from dignitary harm is also fundamental to the defense of their humanity.

## Notes

1. *De Officiis*, I, 30.

2. See "Speech on Behalf of Publius Sestius"; also *De Oratore*.

3. *Essays, Civil and Moral* (Cambridge: Harvard Classics, 1909–14).

4. *The doctrine & discipline of divorce* (London: [s.n], 1644), p. 2.

5. *Scriptum super libros Sententiarium*, Book III, distinction 35, question 1, article 4, solution 1c.

6. All encyclicals quoted were retrieved from the Vatican website in official translations. Paragraph numbers are in the originals.

7. *Scriptum super libros Sententiarium*, Book III, distinction 35, question 1, article 4, solution 1c.

8. "A Note on Measuring Well-Being," in *Summary Measures of Population Health*, ed. C. J. L. Murray (Geneva: World Health Organization, 2002), p. 131.

9. Ruth Macklin, "Editorial: Dignity Is a Useless Concept," *British Medical Journal* 327 (2003): 1419–20.

10. *New York Review of Books*, March 27, 1997.

11. New Haven: Yale University Press, 2000.

# Aristocratic Dignity?

## Don Herzog

On the academic lectern, too, we've leveled up. We're interested in good arguments, no matter how base or despicable other cultures might have imagined the speaker. If there still are a lot of white guys in universities, no one takes seriously the claim that universities are theirs by right.

But it would be mistaken to imagine the lectern (or for that matter the public sphere) as a place for nothing but the bloodless give-and-take of reasons. It also is a site for jousting, for thrusts and parries, cutting objections, and even sneers—for the nerd's version of a duel. So I shall have to begin by disappointing sanguinary readers: it is always a pleasure to read and listen to Waldron. Then too, I am entirely sympathetic to his approach to human dignity: I think that modeling our moral understanding on the legal categories is quite promising.

Don't worry, I have some reservations. But mostly what I want to do is continue further down the same path. Here's the nub of what I'm after: aristocratic dignity, like the academic lectern, has attractive features. But it also has decidedly unattractive features. These features are themselves deeply embedded in modern law. They are embedded, too, more broadly in morality and everyday social life. I think Waldron is missing how much reconstruction aristocratic dignity needs to do the work he wants it to.

So: the Countess of Rutland, Waldron tells us, enjoyed a couple of remarkable legal privileges. She couldn't be bodily seized or jailed for debt. Now we all enjoy those privileges. There's a lovely case of leveling up.

But compare: In 1573 England, John Fortescue had a problem. His neighbor, Lord Grey de Wilton, liked to go hunting—and trespass on land in which Fortescue had the right of free warren. Fortescue complained repeatedly. The lord's jaunty response? "Stuffe a turd in your teethe," he told his neighbor. "I will hunt it, and it shall be hunted in spite of all you can do."[1] There were Star Chamber proceedings between the two.[2] Grey ambushed Fortescue and beat him, knocking him off his horse. Fortescue was no ordinary commoner: he was a member of Parliament and would go on to become chancellor of the exchequer. Queen Elizabeth's displeasure with Grey led the poor lord to spend some time in Fleet Prison.

So much for dispute resolution, claim and counterclaim, and reason-giving among the dignified. But it's worse than that. Grey's "turd in your teeth" would have been exactly right had he been addressing any ordinary commoner. Yes, England offered aristocrats fewer formal legal privileges than did the rest of Europe. But even in England, peers of the realm couldn't be arrested except for treason, felony, and breach of the peace. They couldn't be forced to appear in court on most writs. They didn't have to testify under oath: how insulting not to take their word for it! No wonder a 1648 petition to the House of Commons (and there are others like it) implored them to make "Kings, Queens, Princes, Dukes, Earls, Lords, and all persons, alike liable to every law of the land...so all persons even the Highest might fear and stand in aw, and neither violate the publick peace, nor private right of person or estate, (as hath been frequent) without being lyable to accompt as other men."[3]

Here's Edward Hyde, later Earl of Clarendon, addressing the House of Commons in 1640:

He told them another Story as ridiculous, of a Gentleman, who, owing his Taylor a long Time a good Sum of Money for Cloaths, and his Taylor coming one Day to his Chamber, with more than ordinary Importunity for his Debt, and not receiving any good Answer, threatened to arrest him; upon which the Gentleman, enraged, gave him very ill Words, called him base Fellow, and laid his hands upon him to thrust him out of his chamber: in this Struggle, and under this Provocation, Oppression, and Reproach, the poor Taylor chanced to say, that He was as good a Man as the other; for which Words He was called into the Marshal's Court; and for his Peace, was content to be satisfied his Debt, out of his own ill Manners; being compelled to release all his other Demands in Lieu of Damages.[4]

I offer these vignettes not to produce a few stray details from the rich and repellent history of the British aristocracy, nor so that you can join a campaign to reintroduce "a turd in your teeth" into everyday use. Instead, I want the example to set up this point: at the heart of the dignity enjoyed by aristocrats was the claim, "I don't have to answer to the likes of you." That claim, which took specific legal form, is deeply antithetical to the version of dignity Waldron wants to tease out, and again it's deeply entrenched. So we need to do two things. We need to get it into focus. Then we need to think about what kind of work needs to be done to reconstruct noble dignity so it can do the work we want it to. It may be that we face more work than just paring off the bad parts.

First things first: let's focus. Take the canonical form for royal proclamations: "it is our royal pleasure…" Or take the form of royal assent for signing a bill from Britain's Parliament into law, a typically bastardized bit of law-French: "*la Reyne le veult,*" or the queen wills it. Today this is mere verbal form. Once it was real, and it underlined that mere will or even caprice was enough. Here we have authority exercised without even a shred of a pretense that it is reasoned judgment. So Shakespeare's Henry V starts a war with France because he's insulted by a gag with some tennis balls and stops it because he falls in love with Catherine of Valois. The poor subjects of the realm careen around at his whim.

Or take the advice another seventeenth-century aristocrat, the Earl of Derby, offered his son: "Undertake no suit against a poor man...for then you make him your equal."[5] Listen to Charles I, demanding money from Parliament in 1628: "Take not this as a threatning (for I scorn to threaten any but my equals)."[6] That same year, at the election at Lewes, the gentry found it degrading to have their names on the same electoral rolls as those of the enfranchised commoners, so they refused to vote.[7] Two centuries later, the same sensibility surfaced in frenzied Tory complaints about the Reform Bill of 1832. Here's Sir Charles Wetherell, addressing the House of Commons during the bill's second reading, July 6, 1831:

A more rash and tyrannical innovation on the constitution than the present had, he said, never been attempted,—the tendency of the measure was to democratize, he had almost said to *sansculottize* the constitution. The ten pound voters were a mere mockery of a representative body. He ventured to assert it as a proposition in the abstract, that ten pound men were not fit for the enjoyment of the elective franchise. What! he would ask the gentlemen opposite, was this their conservative body? the respectable constituency of the parish workhouse! For his part, he considered that to solicit votes in the lazaretto—in pauper establishments—was degrading to the character, qualifications, and station of a representative.[8]

Wetherell was recorder of Bristol. When he showed up there a few months after delivering himself of this genial sentiment, he was met with jeers and stones. When he offered to imprison those responsible, riots began. By the end, buildings lay in smoking rubble and a dozen were dead—no doubt confirming Wetherell's jaundiced estimate of the lower orders.

The good news for Waldron's thesis is that law was already a realm for the give-and-take of reasons and arguments, justifications and criticisms, among dignified equals. The bad news is that that is precisely why the nobility often wanted nothing to do with it. How unseemly to be shoved into a position where you had to answer to the base underlings!

Let me revisit the legal tagline Waldron approvingly adduces: "An Englishman's home is his castle." That, too, might seem to have an endearingly lofty ring about it: your home might be modest, might even be a dump, but in it you're an aristocrat. The reality is rather less charming. Coke echoes a series of late sixteenth- and early seventeenth-century commentators in finding here legal license to use armed, even deadly, force against intruders.[9] But this too is a kind of unaccountability. Without the common law's now familiar enquiry into whether the man defending his house had a reasonable belief that his (or some other occupant's) life or limb was threatened, the unaccountability is stark: the state will not second-guess his judgment about what kind of force he needed to use.

More dramatically, the state's jurisdiction, the reach of the law, stops at the threshold. Through early modernity, the standard view was that the government ruled not over individuals but over male heads of households. This view was formally reaffirmed by the revolutionary assembly in France. A man's house is his castle because inside it, he rules as absolute sovereign. A special dignity for him— and indignity, and helplessness, for others. I suspect, though I don't have enough evidence up my sleeve to be confident, that this view, rather more than the fact of the marriage contract, explains why the law found it so hard to frame marital rape as a crime. Here, by the way, liberal individualism shouldn't be condemned as sociologically naive or pernicious. It should be embraced as offering legal recourse and dignity to those on the other side of the threshold, once invisible.

So again, at the core of the legal dignity enjoyed by aristocrats is something like this: I enjoy special privileges and need not answer to the likes of you for how I use them. *That* is not something we have made available to everyone. Nor is it something we should. But that core still shows up, curiously, in modern law, notwithstanding all our commitments to liberalism, democracy, equality, the rule of law, and the like.

I don't mean qualified or even absolute privileges that we justify as instrumentally required to get a job done. The Constitution, for instance, says that "for any Speech or Debate in either House," senators and representatives "shall not be questioned in any other Place."[10] On the floor, your senator can slander you to his heart's content. The language will be published in the *Congressional Record*. And you won't be able to sue him. Why? Because we want to be sure to preserve robust debate. But those kinds of privileges are connected to what Waldron calls condition status. No surprise that when William Proxmire was sued for lambasting the recipient of one of his Golden Fleece Awards off the floor of the Senate, he didn't enjoy immunity.[11]

What about Florida's embrace of the so-called castle doctrine? This statute overturns long-standing common law.[12] Suppose you're in your house or other dwelling, or even your car, and someone is "unlawfully and forcefully entering." You may use deadly force against him and Florida will presume that you had a reasonable fear of death or great bodily harm, which will then excuse your action as self-defense. For today's purposes, I don't care if you cheer or deplore this legal innovation. And it is, for sure, universal. But what it extends is "I can kill someone in my house and I needn't answer for it." In this way, Florida has made its homeowners, apartment-dwellers, and even drivers aristocrats for a day—or, I suppose, not for any particular time, but any time at all when they're in their special castles. I won't be surprised if courts try to haul the statute back toward the common law. But it's worth remembering that plenty of public celebration of Florida's act depended on the cruder thought that you should be free to kill intruders. It's worth remembering too that state after state is adopting similar legislation.

Or consider the bizarre doctrine of state sovereign immunity. The Eleventh Amendment to the Constitution says that a citizen of one state can't sue another state in federal court. In 1887, the Supreme Court said this was a matter of dignity: "The very object and purpose of the 11th amendment were to prevent the indignity of subjecting a State to the coercive process of judicial tribunals at the instance of private parties."[13] In 1890, the Supreme Court held that individuals can't sue states, period, even if they are citizens of that very state: "It is inherent in the nature of sovereignty not to be amenable to the suit of an individual without its consent."[14] (So much for the dictates of plain text!) This law is alive and well. Writing for the Court in 2002, Justice Thomas insisted, "The preeminent purpose of state sovereign immunity is to accord States the dignity that is consistent with their status as sovereign entities."[15] Yes, states may graciously deign to let their citizens sue them. But nothing requires them to waive immunity. If they choose not to, they can exult in their legal dignity and say to you, stuff a turd in your teeth. The putative justifications sometimes offered for sovereign immunity are quite obviously threadbare. So, we're sometimes told, the state is busy with important tasks and has better things to do than answer lawsuits. The same might be said of General Motors. Or again, we're sometimes reminded that finally taxpayers foot the bill of lawsuits, so "we" would be suing "ourselves." But if you sue GM for selling you a defective car that got you hurt in an accident, we don't bar the suit if we learn that you're a shareholder in the corporation. And yes, I know that some of us are weirdly inclined to treat corporations with the same deference some are inclined to treat governments.

Better, as usual, not to lose ourselves in the abstractions. What does sovereign immunity mean on the ground? In April 2005, Susan Birk gave birth to her daughter, Vayle. The infant needed emergency surgery and she needed it in a hurry. The transport team showed up eighty minutes later than they said they would. That lost time meant everything: Vayle suffered "severe, permanent brain damage, among other things." Pursuant to Connecticut law, Birk and her husband, acting for Vayle, sought permission to sue the state—the medical facilities screwing up were public. The claims commissioner rejected her claim because she hadn't filed some of the relevant paperwork. The family then sought to reopen the claim, the commissioner agreed to let them sue—and then a state court said no, he had no legal authority to reopen the case. So the state would remain legally immune, in a setting where private parties would have been paying millions of dollars.[16]

Some critics think it's conceptually confused to attribute dignity to states. I think that's wrong: it depends on a bankrupt methodological individualism that somehow passes for hardheaded wisdom these days, though I haven't space to attack the view here. Anyway I think the view that states have dignity—or, better, the sort of dignity that means they can sniff disdainfully and refuse to answer citizens' complaints in courts of law—is perfectly coherent. It's just repellent, an affront to the rule of law. In this way, our governments enjoy just the kind of legal dignity aristocrats once did. But their being unanswerable for their injuries and affronts is miles away from the vision of dignity Waldron rightly affirms. So it's not enough to say we've leveled up. Human dignity has to be more than offering everyone the kind of legal dignity once enjoyed by aristocrats. It has to reconstruct or reject that dignity because we have no interest in casting dignity as the haughty business of behaving badly and refusing to be held accountable for it. "Rank has its privileges": that is the loathsome underbelly, or maybe prominently displayed belly, of the noble dignity Waldron is embracing.

* * *

Before I gesture toward how a reconstruction might go, I have two sneers for you. (No, not *at* you.)

The first is from Jeremy Bentham advising Greek legislators in 1823. "Never is the day labourer, never is the helpless pauper, an object of contempt to me: I can not say the same thing of the purse-proud aristocrat: I can not say the same thing of the ancestry-proud aristocrat: I can not say the same thing of the official bloodsucker: I can not say the same thing of the man covered with the tokens of factitious honor: least of all can I say the same of a King."[17]

The second is recorded by the poet Thomas Moore six years later. Its victim is Robert Peel, the great Tory who would become prime minister. Peel's father had gotten fabulously wealthy in textiles, so poor Peel, nouveau riche that he was, had, as Moore reports others felt, "vulgar manners." "This, it seems, is a favourite subject of merriment with the King, who sometimes says 'Now, I shall call Peel over to me—watch him, as he comes—he can't even walk like a gentleman'—These people, in their insolence, attribute this want of gentleman-like air in Peel to his birth. As if some of the highest among themselves had not the looks & minds of *waiters*."[18] Yes, there's a sneer in there at waiters, but that's not the one I want— yet. I want you to ponder the king and his merry little band of aristocrats, obnoxious gods from Mount Olympus, toying with and belittling poor Peel, chuckling at his awkward gait, banding together as superiors who cement their dignified status by having ridiculous underlings around and rejoicing in their ridiculousness.

These sneers are glimpses of a long-running cultural war over contempt and therefore over dignity. Waldron affectionately quotes Robert Burns's verse, with its endearing refrain, "A man's a man for a' that." That one gives you the benign picture of leveling up: hey, we're not low-lifes, we're every bit as dignified as the nobility. Bentham's sneer is different. It inverts the usual status hierarchy. Bentham has no contempt for workers and paupers: they're dignified figures. But he says he does have contempt for aristocrats and kings. Indeed, he boasts about it. It's as if the only way to be dignified is to scorn the credentials of the well-born.

So Bentham sneers at the king and the king sneers at Peel. No one here has the idea of meeting as dignified equals. It's only a question of who's on top. This cultural war is long-running—indeed, it's not over—and it's fought on many fronts. It's fought out in august moments of public law, such as the French revolutionary assembly somberly voting to strip France's aristocrats of one privilege after another. It's fought out in episode after episode in private law, such as what sorts of cuffs and beatings will and won't be actionable in tort instead of privileged as discipline. It's fought out in the nitty-gritty scenes of everyday life, where we struggle over flared nostrils; deliberate shoves and inadvertent ones, too; respectful eye contact, unpleasantly prolonged stares, and that particular, peculiar kind of blithe disregard that involves looking straight through somebody. And it has other moments of startling inversion, such as commoners dueling to boost their social status.[19]

Here dignity isn't readily available to one and all. People are scuffling for it and an ever-tempting way to climb the ladder of dignity is to push others down. It's a mistake to think that dignity is necessarily what economists call a positional good. But often it has been. Often it still is. I'm absolutely with Waldron in seeking an account of human dignity that makes it available to one and all. But that means positional accounts of dignity, ones depending on exalted position over the base underlings, aren't merely unattractive. They're nonstarters as a matter of logic. Those are my two sneers and those are their stakes.

Next I want to introduce a distinction in social theory. Waldron offers some sensible ways of thinking about the concept of status. Here's another one—anyway I hope it's sensible—which depends on contrasting it with the idea of a social role. Let's say that your status follows you across the whole social landscape. Aristocratic status is like that. You're a duke not only when you proudly survey your dominions; not only when you assure your impoverished tenants that you'll instruct your agent to be less harsh with them about making payments; and not only when you promenade at court in your ermine robes, drink too much sherry, and grope the servant maids. You're a duke 24/7, as we might say today. You require special treatment no matter where you are, no matter what you're doing. In church you will sit in a grand pew at the front. In Parliament you will be entitled to a seat in the House of Lords. The tailor will come to your estate and if he dares to demand that you pay your debts, you'll have your way with him, socially and legally, for his audacity. If for some reason you appear in the marketplace, others will bow low or even fawn and scrape, make way for you, and ask what you want in submissive tones they don't use for any old customer. And so on.

But a role is just a position in some institution. So it's something you ordinarily shift in and out of, unless you're unlucky enough to be captive of one of Erving Goffman's total institutions. Writing or delivering these comments, I'm a professor. I suppose there's a sense in which I'm a professor when I'm grocery shopping—it's still my job—and sometimes my younger daughter teases me about my unimpeachable claims to expertise in jazz by saying, "Oh, right, you're a *law professor*," words she draws out with comically ironical awe. But—trust me—I don't quote Bentham at the supermarket. And I suppose you don't open your laptops and take notes on the dinner conversation when you're visiting your family. When Bill Ford, great-grandson of Henry and then CEO of Ford, showed up at a dinner meeting at my daughter's elementary school, he grabbed the same paper plates and plastic utensils the rest of us did, he stood in line with the rest of us, and he ate the same gloppy food. And a damned good thing: he was there as parent of a student, not as CEO. We no longer imagine society as one unified hierarchy. Because of social differentiation—the emergence of a host of largely autonomous institutions—that view has become empirically implausible. Instead we see a series of institutions—states, economic firms, families, universities, Boy Scout troops, you name it—with reasonably clear jurisdictional boundaries.

It is a feature, not a bug, of Waldron's account that human dignity is in this way a status. It follows us around relentlessly: or anyway we want it to and think it should. We may need to punish criminals. But it is still cause for grave concern, even horror, when we gratuitously humiliate them, let alone torture them. We don't want to crush their dignity. So, too, our bodies may betray us. We may become incontinent. We may drool uncontrollably or twitch badly or shuffle along hunched over and hesitantly instead of walking upright and briskly. But there is something worrisome about people who mock or flinch at what we rightly describe as these indignities, let alone those tone-deaf buffoons who sneer at the very idea of death with dignity. No matter what our social or biological plight, we are entitled to dignity. So I think the distinction between status and role brings out a decided merit of Waldron's account: it highlights the crucial fact that our dignity doesn't simply attach to particular roles. The relevant sense of dignity here is not the sort you forfeit by slipping on a banana peel or lecturing with your fly unzipped or anything like that. Indeed, at stake in Waldron's concern with how we treat criminals is that you can't forfeit this kind of dignity even by grotesque immorality. That is, criminals still have claims on how we may and may not treat them: no abuse, no torture, no officially sponsored or officially neglected rape. That we flout these claims on a daily, ongoing, bureaucratized basis depends in part on a kind of aristocratic contempt for the underlings.

It is then another feature, not a bug, of Waldron's account that it helps explain and justify why we worry endlessly about gender, race, social class, sexual orientation, and the like. For these, too, seem to work as social statuses. And, depending of course on what status you occupy, they may open you up to indignity after indignity. I have nothing nice to say about the jargon and canting of much work in the humanities these days. But concerns about these matters are not in fact the hangover of the 1960s or the special preoccupation of tenured radicals. Try this, from Mary Wollstonecraft's best book, her observations on Scandinavia:

In fact, the situation of the servants in every respect, particularly that of the women, shews how far the swedes are from having a just conception of rational equality. They are not *termed* slaves; yet a man may strike a man with impunity because he pays him wages; though these wages are so low, that necessity must teach them to pilfer, whilst servility renders them false and boorish. Still the men stand up for the dignity of man, by oppressing the women. The most menial, and even laborious offices, are therefore left to these poor drudges. Much of this I have seen. In the winter, I am told, they take the linen down to the river, to wash it in the cold water; and though their hands, cut by the ice, are cracked and bleeding, the men, their fellow servants, will not disgrace their manhood by carrying a tub to lighten their burden.[20]

Even among the wretched servants, the men propped up their dignity by mistreating the women. Wollstonecraft already knew the personal and private were political.

Is domestic service itself a hateful affront to human dignity? By 1699, *catch fart* had passed into the English language, at least the colorful version of it spoken by deviants, as slang for a footboy.[21] (And this, alas, after I ruminated on "stuff a turd in your teeth." This is my plot to clinch the award for most scatological Tanner commentator.) It was still in use at the end of the eighteenth century, and one dictionary spells out the point: "CATCH FART. A footboy; so called from such servants commonly following close behind their master or mistress."[22] Whether a footboy can be dignified, whether any number of so-called menial occupations can be dignified, what we should make of Thomas Moore's sneer that some aristocrats have manners no better than those of waiters: all this raises struggles over the dignity of labor whose pursuit would take me too far afield. I'd notice only that when devoted service becomes one's only task—when we're talking about live-in servants with no serious time off to pursue other activities, to occupy other roles—it's harder to see it as dignified. Why? Because then one's identity threatens to collapse all the way into the job.

James Boswell feasted on the same gender dynamics that made Wollstonecraft's gorge rise. Take this 1762 journal entry:

Indeed, in my mind, there cannot be higher felicity on earth enjoyed by man than the participation of genuine reciprocal amorous affection with an amiable woman. There he has a full indulgence of all the delicate feelings and pleasures both of body and mind, while at the same time in this enchanting union he exults with a consciousness that he is the superior person. The dignity of his sex is kept up.[23]

If the dignity of his sex is kept up by romantic affection and sexual intercourse, the dignity of hers is kept down. For both Wollstonecraft and Boswell, to be male is to be something of an aristocrat. Wollstonecraft condemns the fact; Boswell embraces it. Here, too, we find the motif I focused on earlier: the exercise of exclusive privileges for which one needn't answer to the underlings. Boswell kept his endless assignations with prostitutes and others secret from his wife, but that seems to have been a matter of prudently avoiding domestic conflict, not any acknowledgment that what he was doing was wrong. He'd not have had the same stance about any infidelity of hers.

So we have the idea of a valuable status, human dignity, that you don't relinquish, no matter what social setting you find yourself in. This means that dignity can't be a wholesale attack on status. But we also have the idea of inferior or base statuses, some of them the sort that Goffman identified as stigma, that you don't relinquish, either. We'd like to get rid of those in the name of human dignity. Not any old status will do, and as you now know, I am skeptical of the claim that aristocratic status is what we're after.

So status is crucial. But I think we can get some more purchase on the idea of dignity by thinking about roles. In any given social setting, we're selectively forgetful: we ignore considerations irrelevant to the business at hand. When you go to vote in a primary, it may matter whether you're a Republican or a Democrat. But it doesn't matter whether you're a Catholic or a Jew or an atheist, whether you root for the Boston Red Sox or the New York Yankees, whether you are an especially loving parent or happen to have no children. When you go to buy vegetables at the market, you don't ordinarily care about the religion or politics of the seller. (Whether the crops are organic might be a political issue, but that's not the sense of *politics* at issue here.) There's a kind of equality in this and also a kind of dignity: you might be thought badly of in some other setting, but you leave its concerns behind when you take up a new role.

We can use the law to model this strand of dignity, too. Justice is blind: not that judges are tottering and decrepit, but that the law will resolutely ignore all kinds of facts that might in some other social setting be perfectly relevant. If English law once had special rules to recognize aristocratic status, it also came, sometimes at least, to ignore and so flout that status. Here's Bentham again, this time from some of his scribbled notes on French reforms of judicial procedure:

What then? Are men of the first rank and consideration—are men high in office—men whose time is not less valuable to the public than to themselves—are such men to be forced to quit their business, their functions, or what is more than all, their pleasure, at the beck of every idle or malicious adversary, to dance attendance upon every petty cause? Yes, as far as it is necessary, they and everybody. What if, instead of parties, they were witnesses? Upon business of other people's everybody is obliged to attend, and nobody complains of it. Were the Prince of Wales, the Archbishop of Canterbury, and the Lord High Chancellor, to be passing by in the same coach, while a chimney-sweeper and a barrow-woman were in dispute about a halfpennyworth of apples, and the chimney-sweeper or the barrow-woman were to think proper to call upon them for their evidence, could they refuse it? No, most certainly.[24]

A "great man," Bentham went on, might well find talking to attorneys and testifying before judges "humiliating to his grandeur," but no matter. Like it or not, he would have to participate in legal proceedings. Bentham's "nobody complains of it" is facetious whistling in the dark. He knew full well that aristocrats and other Pooh-Bahs were enraged by the law's commitment to equality, its cheerfully ignoring their august status and putting them on level playing fields with such ignoble types as chimney sweeps.

It is painfully obvious that the law doesn't live up to its own ideal of equality, that justice all too regularly peeks out from behind her blindfold, that race and class and political power can make all the difference even when they're entirely irrelevant. So, too, it is painfully obvious that role differentiation more generally doesn't live up to its own structures of equality. We know that the rich have more political power, not just more market goodies. You may have suspected that white men do better on the market. Well, empirical studies have shown that white men get offered better prices on cars and do better in bargaining compared with women and minorities with the same economic profiles.[25] Let's not even get started about what happens if you're particularly good-looking—or particularly not. About such lamentable everyday leakage across roles, institutions, and their jurisdictional boundaries, about the ongoing influence of baleful status categories, I am inclined to say just what Waldron does. There is a normative order here and when our actual practices don't live up to their own aspirations, we know what's wrong and we can struggle to improve things.

So where are we? To make sense of human dignity, we need to hang on to the *form* of status, understood as something that travels with you everywhere you go, not just a role you occupy now and again. But law's blindness to irrelevant facts, its brushing aside the *content* of lots of status claims as irrelevant to the matter at hand, is one of our most powerful images of equality—and of dignity. Just think of Bentham's chimney sweep issuing a subpoena to the duke. Waldron is right, too, in urging that we need more than mere form: we want to illuminate the fact that everyone enjoys a high status, not just that everyone now has the same status. I am happy to agree that some of the content of aristocratic status is helpful: again, recall the Countess of Rutland's enjoying the special privileges not to be seized or jailed for debt and how we've now extended that to everyone. But too much of what aristocrats had, in law and society, is stuff we want to abolish, not extend to everyone. We don't want even furtively to embrace having special perks and not answering to others for your mistreatment of them. And again, desirability aside, we can't coherently embrace anything positional.

So what else can we say about the content of human dignity? I'm a fox, not a hedgehog: I rather doubt there is one big imposing thing to say about such topics. I suppose my rejection of much of noble dignity and privilege might seem a rejection of Waldron's central thesis. But I'd rather see it as a partial emptying out of Waldron's view. I think we can still go far by thinking about how the law treats people. I am wholly in agreement, for instance, with Waldron's suggestion that the law credits us with self-command, and that that is an ascription of dignity. I shall underline, what he does not, that command theories of law are then deeply defective—as if we were terrified privates confronted with a sadistic sergeant in basic training.

I want to close with yet another quotation. I hope you'll forgive me not just for its length but also for not delicately skipping over the excruciating language it contains. (Squirming or breaking a sweat or flushing with anger at this language, I note polemically, isn't a sign of mindless PC orthodoxy; it is a visceral sign of our commitment to human dignity.) It is one of my favorite stories about human dignity. Thomas de Quincey says he got this story from William Hazlitt, the fabulous essayist, staunch democrat, and garden-variety misogynist. Anyway, the Duke of Cumberland is out for a walk:

His Royal Highness had rooms in St. James's; and one day, as he was issuing from the palace into Pall-Mall, Hazlitt happened to be immediately behind him: he could therefore watch his motions along the whole line of his progress. It is the custom in England, wheresoever the persons of the royal family are familiar to the public eye, as at Windsor, &c., that all passengers in the street, on seeing them, walk bare-headed, or make some signal of dutiful respect. On this occasion all the men who met the prince took off their hats, the prince acknowledging every such obeisance by a separate bow. Pall-Mall being finished, and its whole harvest of royal salutations gathered in, next the Duke came to Cockspur Street. But here, and taking a station close to the crossing, which daily he beautified and polished with his broom, stood a negro sweep. If human at all,—which some people doubted,—he was pretty nearly as abject a representative of our human family divine as can ever have existed. Still he was held to be a man by the law of the land; which would have hanged any person, gentle or simple, for cutting his throat. Law (it is certain) conceived him to be a man, however poor a one, though medicine, in an under-tone, muttered sometimes a demur to that opinion. But here the sweep was, whether man or beast, standing humbly in the path of royalty: vanish he would not; he was (as the Times says of the Corn League) "a great fact," if rather a muddy one; and, though, by his own confession (repeated one thousand times a-day), both "a nigger" and a sweep, ("Remember poor nigger, your honour! remember poor sweep!"), yet the creature could take off his rag of a hat and earn the bow of a prince as well as any white native of St. James's. What was to be done? A great case of conscience was on the point of being raised in the person of a paralytic nigger; nay, possibly a state question.—Ought a son of England, could a son of England, descend from his majestic pedestal to gild with the rays of his condescension such a grub, such a very doubtful grub, as this? Total Pall-Mall was sagacious of the coming crisis; judgment was going to be delivered; a precedent to be raised; and Pall-Mall stood still, with Hazlitt at its head, to learn the issue. How if the black should be a Jacobin, and (in the event of the duke's bowing) should have a bas-relief sculptured on his tomb exhibiting an English prince and a German king as two separate personages in the act of worshiping his broom? Luckily it was not the black's province to settle the case. The Duke of Cumberland, seeing no counsel at hand to argue either the pro or the contra, found himself obliged to settle the question de piano; so, drawing out his purse, he kept his hat as rigidly settled on his head as William Penn and Mead did before the Recorder of London. All Pall-Mall applauded; contradicente Gulielmo Hazlitt, and Hazlitt only. The black swore that the prince gave him half-a-crown; but whether he regarded this in the light or a godsend to his avarice or a shipwreck to his ambition—whether he was more thankful for the money gained, or angry for the honour lost—did not transpire. "No matter," said Hazlitt; "the black might be a fool; but I insist upon it that he was entitled to the bow, since all Pall-Mall had it before him, and that it was unprincely to refuse it."[26]

There's legal equality here, and hurray for that. But if we're tempted to model human dignity, as a moral and finally a social ideal, on aristocratic dignity, we're going to have to think hard about the duke's offering money (maybe) but not a bow, and why the crowd approved, and why Hazlitt didn't. I think finally we're going to have to adopt Hazlitt's sensibility here as our own and think about how sadly comfortable we remain with aristocratic deference, with receiving it, offering it, extorting it, and—whether we are on the receiving or offering end—basking in it.

But notice, finally, how Hazlitt voices his complaint: he says the duke's snub was unprincely. An intriguing bit of leveling up is available here, and this bit, I'm happy to say, fits Waldron's central thesis perfectly: we can help undergird human dignity by universalizing the easy grace and civility of the best aristocrats.

## Notes

1. Lawrence Stone, *The Crisis of the Aristocracy, 1558–1641* (Oxford: Clarendon, 1965), p. 236.

2. *Fortescue v. Legrey*, STAC 5/F24/31.

3. *To the Right Honovrable the Commons of England in Parliament Assembled* (n.p., [1648]).

4. *The Life of Edward Earl of Clarendon* (Oxford, 1759), p. 37.

5. Barry Reay, "Quaker Opposition to Tithes 1652–1660," *Past & Present*, February 1980, pp. 98–120, p. 114.

6. *Ephemeris Parliamentaria, or A Faithfull Record of the Transactions in Parliament* (London, 1654), p. 2.

7. Derek Hirst, *The Representative of the People? Voters and Voting in England under the Early Stuarts* (Cambridge: Cambridge University Press, 1975), p. 14.

8. "The Late Debate on Reform," *Blackwood's Edinburgh Magazine* 30:183 (August 1831): 398. Compare the more extended and less inflammatory account in "Reform Bill, Second Reading," *The Cabinet Annual Register* (London, 1832), 1:101.The most extended report, including the gem about the lazaretto, is in *Hansard's Parliamentary Debates*, 3rd ser., vol. 4 (1831), starting at II:852.

9. William Lambard, *Eirenarcha: or of The Office of the Justices of Peace in Foure Bookes, Gathered 1579: First Published 1581: and Now Secondly Reuised, Corrected, and Enlarged* (London, 1592), p. 248; *Semayne's Case*, 5 Co. Rep. 91a, 77 Eng. Rep. 194 (K. B. 1604), opinion by Coke, at pp. 91b, 195; Guilliaulme Staundford, *Les Plees del Corone* (London, 1607), pp. 14 recto, 15 verso; Edw[ard] Coke, *The Third Part of the Institutes of the Laws of England* (London, 1644), pp. 161–62.

10. Art. 1, sec. 6.

11. *Hutchinson v. Proxmire*, 443 U.S. 111 (1979).

12. Fla. Stat. §§ 776.012, 776.013.

13. *In re Ayers*, 123 U.S. 443 (1887), 505.

14. *Hans v. Louisiana*, 134 U.S. 1 (1890), 13.

15. *Federal Maritime Commission v. South Carolina Ports Authority*, 535 U.S. 743 (2002), 760.

16. *Nelson v. Dettmer*, 2008 Conn. Super.LEXIS 2853.

17. "Jeremy Bentham to Greek Legislators," in Bentham, *Securities against Misrule and Other Constitutional Writings for Tripoli and Greece*, ed. Philip Schofield (Oxford: Clarendon Press, 1990), p. 194.

18. *The Journal of Thomas Moore*, ed. Wilfred S. Dowden et al., 6 vols. (Newark: University of Delaware Press, 1983–91), 3:1189–90 (February 18, 1829).

19. Mika LaVaque-Manty, "Dueling for Equality: Masculine Honor and the Modern Politics of Dignity," *Political Theory* 34:6 (December 2006): 715–40.

20. Mary Wollstonecraft, *Letters Written during a Short Residence in Sweden, Norway, and Denmark* (London, 1796), p. 27.

21. B. E., *A New Dictionary of the Terms Ancient and Modern of the Canting Crew* (London, [1699]), s.v. *catch-fart*.

22. [Francis Grose,] *A Classical Dictionary of the Vulgar Tongue*, 3rd edition (London, 1796), s.v. *Catch Fart*.

23. *Boswell's London Journal 1762–1763*, ed. Frederick A. Pottle (New York: McGraw-Hill, 1950), p. 84 (December 14, 1762).

24. "Bentham's Draught for the Organization of Judicial Establishments, Compared with That of the National Assembly, with a Commentary on the Same," in *The Works of Jeremy Bentham*, ed. John Bowring, 11 vols. (Edinburgh, 1843), 4:320–21.

25. Ian Ayres, "Fair Driving: Gender and Race Discrimination in Retail Car Negotiations," *Harvard Law Review* 104 (February 1991): 817–72; Ayres, "Further Evidence of Discrimination in New Car Negotiations and Estimates of Its Cause," *Michigan Law Review* 94 (October 1995): 109–46.

26. *The Collected Writings of Thomas de Quincey*, ed. David Masson, 14 vols. (Edinburgh, 1889–90), 11:348–49.

# High and Low

WAI CHEE DIMOCK

I'd like to respond to two impulses in Jeremy Waldron's lectures that seem to be pulling in two slightly different directions. One is the impulse to provide housing for the concept of dignity, to claim it as a foundation for jurisprudence. The other is the impulse to put this house on a very high level, a platform that represents an averaging up, an elevation to the nobility of rank even for the common citizen. What Waldron is proposing, then, would seem not only to be a common denominator, but a very high one. While this is not necessarily a contradiction, it does seem to me to be a difficult level for human beings to stay on for long. I'd like to come back to this, and link this elevated ideal to one particular genre, tragedy, which also happens to be a "high" genre. And I'll ask whether this is a sustainable (or desirable) height for everyone, whether—to balance things out—we might not also want to consider a comic supplement, a common denominator adjusted significantly downwards, paired with a jurisprudence that aspires to be nontragic.

For now, though, I'd like to concentrate on the first question, namely, housing, or where to put the concept of dignity, where to locate its proper home. Since the objection has sometimes been made that this concept is too broad and ill-defined to be a legal concept, Waldron is emphatic in saying that this is not the case. Dignity, for him, not only belongs within the precincts of law, it is central to law's inner workings, a cornerstone for its conception of humanity. It shouldn't have just an incidental or "retail" relation to law, but an across-the-board, fully binding, and indeed "wholesale" relation.

I am sympathetic to Waldron's attempt to work out a jurisprudence with a nontrivial philosophical base, extending the privilege of rank to those who have not been traditionally granted that privilege. I am especially struck by his discussion of dignity as an internal mechanism of self-application and self-monitoring, a style of enforcement that distinguishes the rule of law from being a purely coercive instrumentality, different, in his words, from "herding cows with a cattle prod." I am struck, as well, by his discussion of dignity as a working concept providing law with pragmatic standards such as "reasonable care" or "reasonable speed," which take the average behavior of the common citizen and generalize it into a legal norm.

In all these ways, law does seem a good home for the concept of dignity. I wonder, however, if Waldron wants to argue that the concept is not only fully in residence here but also advantageously native, that this home is not just one among others, but the birthplace, the genetic ground for the concept, enjoying a priority shared by none other. If so, is its appearance in other fields more or less epiphenomenal, a secondary or second-order occurrence, a side effect of its prior grounding in law?

I ask because the concept of dignity shows up not just in moral philosophy but also, quite regularly, in works of literature. So I'd like to ask Waldron to consider a slight amendment to his model, allowing for multiple habitats, with the concept of dignity circulating freely among them, being differently shaped by each of these different environments, bringing to law competing scenarios that have already been tried out, and, in some cases, amounting to cautionary tales. Professor Waldron has already mentioned the importance of dignity to poets such as William Wordsworth and Robert Burns. I'd like to suggest that what is true of these two might also be true of a broad range of literary phenomena, that this might be an archive worth looking at when we think about where the concept of dignity might take us.

Rather than sticking with poetry, though, I'd like to begin with the novel and follow the trajectory of that word, "dignity," in one of the most canonical works of American literature, Melville's *Moby-Dick*. Significantly, the word appears in a chapter entitled "Knights and Squires." Of course, we know that there are no actual knights and squires on the whaling ship. Melville is only pretending that there are; he is elevating the common seamen to these lofty ranks, treating them as if they could claim the same dignity as titled noblemen. This is his portrait of Starbuck, the first mate:

> But this august dignity I treat of, is not the dignity of kings and robes, but that abounding dignity which has no robed investiture. Thou shalt see it shining in the arm that wields a pick or drives a spike; that democratic dignity, which, on all hands, radiates without end from God Himself! The great God absolute! The center and circumference of all democracy! His omnipresence, our divine equality![1]

I don't need to point out the uncanny parallel between what Professor Waldron is proposing and what Melville is already putting into practice. For this novelist, dignity is also an aristocratic privilege that has to be democratized, to be extended even to the most humble workingman. And this is not just a passing thought, but the underlying compositional philosophy for the entire novel. Given the centrality of dignity as a fully articulated and indeed fully emplotted concept in *Moby-Dick*, I do think we need to take literature seriously as an alternative home, another test site for the concept of dignity. And I mean "alternative" in quite a literal sense, in that this is really a parallel environment, a platform comparable in scope to the jurisdiction of law, but with the scenarios already worked out, the plots already written, and various destinations already arrived at by the concept of dignity. Literature, in this sense, represents a half-imaginary but also half-empirical laboratory for the propositions of law, since what remains a theoretical conjecture in one is already fully executed and fully enacted in the other, played out to the bitter end, and yielding a set of outcomes that should probably have some bearing on the way we try to project the consequences of various legal concepts.

In that spirit, I would like to call attention to the outcome of *Moby-Dick*, to the high aspiration but also the terrible catastrophe that concludes the novel, and that seems to be activated when the prerogatives of noble rank become the claimable rights for everyone, allowing dignity to take precedence over everything else. Dignity is such a high-maintenance concept, Melville seems to be saying, that its upkeep is quite capable of ruining everyone in its path. After all, the "knights and squires" on the whaling ship are all dead by the end of the novel. They are dead primarily because of that sovereign high ground—the lofty program of revenge—set into motion by Captain Ahab, a seaman named after a king from the Old Testament, and who, like ancient kings, would not give an inch when it comes to his sense of high standing and high entitlement, a dominion that, in this case, is imagined to extend to nonhuman creatures as well as human beings. To repair the damage that, he thinks, has been done to his sovereign dignity, Ahab would stop at nothing, certainly not the destruction of the crew of the *Pequod*. In this novel, we see a possible trajectory for the concept of dignity, and it is not one we can afford to ignore. It suggests, at the very least, that the elevation on which the concept operates might not be sustainable for most of us, that its price is exorbitant, bringing harm both to ourselves and often to others.

I'd like to go back to *Moby-Dick*, and read the paragraph that comes immediately after the one we looked at a moment ago, a sequel that Melville puts in place when the high-maintenance concept of dignity exacts its toll:

If, then, to meanest mariners, and renegades and castaways, I shall hereafter ascribe high qualities, though dark; weave round them tragic graces; if even the most mournful, perchance the most abased, among them all, shall at times lift himself to the exalted mounts; if I shall touch that workman's arm with some ethereal light; if I shall spread a rainbow over his disastrous set of sun; then against all mortal critics bear me out in it, thou just Spirit of Equality, which hast spread one royal mantle of humanity over all my kind. Bear me out in it, thou great Democratic God![2]

Here, Melville is still talking about conferring the dignity of
kings and nobles on ordinary people, a royal mantle spread all
around. But for him, these "high qualities" are "dark." Or, if they
come with an "ethereal light," that light turns out to be the after-
glow of a "disastrous set of sun." In short, for Melville, the fierce
light that comes with aristocratic elevation also points to a symmetrical darkness. It seems that dignity, in being a "high" virtue,
is also potentially open to catastrophe, belonging to the genre of
tragedy. In what follows, I'd like to explore this question by way
of Aristotle and the way he links the ending of this most elevated
of genres to the elevated ranks, social as well as psychological, of
its protagonists.

But I'd like to bracket literature and philosophy for a moment,
and go back briefly to what seems to me a contradiction in Waldron's formulation of the concept. This is his substantive definition
of the term:

Dignity has resonances of something like noble bearing....It connotes...self-possession and self-control; self-presentation as someone to
be reckoned with; not being abject, pitiable, distressed, or overly submissive in circumstances of adversity.

In this passage, Professor Waldron seems to be thinking of dignity
primarily as a virtue coming from within and reflecting upon oneself. It is a self-referential virtue, self-executed, an awareness of
one's high standing, leading to a corresponding nobility of demeanor, a cause-and-effect circuit that runs its course within the
compass of a single individual. The key terms here are all reflexive
terms: self-possession, self-control, self-regard. Professor Waldron
seems to be saying that, for there to be dignity, all it takes is for one
person to feel this self-esteem and to give a salient demonstration
of it. Elsewhere in the lectures, though, he seems to be moving away
from this reflexive model. In this alternative conception, dignity is
not just self-executed and self-validating; instead, it is dependent

on the validation rendered by others, the tribute that they pay in acknowledgment of our high standing. Dignity in this sense—as something that requires outside proof, outside backing that has to be supplied by other people—is obviously much more problematic, since it turns the dignified person from an autonomous individual into a relational dependent, a recipient of the respect that he might or might not get.

It is fair to say that this relational dependency is not something that Professor Waldron emphasizes. For the most part, the dignified person in his paradigm is a noble individual who stands tall on his own, rather than an effect of the cushion of regard coming from others, a cushion that can be withdrawn at any moment. Which is also to say that the high platform where Professor Waldron puts dignity is very much an idealized platform. But a nonidealized or even ignoble counternarrative is perhaps always there, lurking just below the threshold, causing trouble, and, I would argue, making the concept tragedy-prone. On that note, I would like to go now to Aristotle, and through him to Homer, who has pointed us in exactly this direction, calling attention to a nontrivial connection between high dignity on the one hand, and its dependency on the regard of others on the other, a typically tragic partnership.

In the *Poetics*, Aristotle divides literature into two, tragedy and comedy, along this crucial differential axis: the degree of elevation of the protagonists. Tragedy (and by this he includes not only drama but also the Homeric epic) is about "noble actions and the actions of noble persons"; it is located on the high end of the spectrum, it is about those who are better than average, "people who are to be taken seriously."[3] Comedy, by contrast, is definitely on the low end, it is about the recipients of our ridicule, our laughter, those who are worse than average.

All of this is well and good, until we remember that the high end is also the tragic end. Soon or later, the world of these lofty beings will come crashing down, and this is the occasion for the "pity and terror" that Aristotle famously associates with tragedy. Why is it that an elevated platform is also the platform where catastrophes happen with some regularity?

Aristotle is silent about how aristocrats behave, and which of their norms of behavior might lead to tragic outcomes. But, filling in the gap, we can easily come up with a list. From "high standing," we might go on to "highfalutin," "high-handed," "being on a high horse," and so on. These forms of behavior also have something to do with dignity, but they are excessive, unseemly, over the top, a high self-esteem that has no corresponding acknowledgment from the world. We can think of this as the ignoble face of dignity: ignoble, because there is just never enough deference out there, and calling for vigilance and even truculence as a result. And yet, this negative profile isn't so different, after all, from the face that is idealized: both take very seriously the burden of being someone to be reckoned with, refusing to back down, taking umbrage easily, and magnifying a personal injury into a right to retaliate. All of these are the recognizable forms of behavior associated with the privilege of rank; they do seem to me to be the precondition for tragedy.

Aristotle would have been familiar with this nonidealized form of dignity. In fact, the *Iliad* opens with the rage of Achilles, a noble person who stands on his dignity, who furiously informs Agamemnon how much he resents the fact that "My honors never equal yours."[4] Achilles has been forced to give up his maiden, Briseis, in order to compensate Agamemnon for what *he* has lost. And Agamemnon adds insult to injury, taunting him with these words: "You are nothing to me—you and your overweening anger!"[5] Achilles now swears an oath to do no fighting and to stand by and watch while the Greek army dies in droves:

> I tell you this, and I swear a mighty oath upon it
> by this, this scepter, look...
> upholding the honored customs whenever Zeus commands—
> This scepter will be the mighty force behind my oath:
> someday, I swear, a yearning for Achilles will strike

Achaea's sons and all your armies! But then, Atrides,
Harrowed as you will be, nothing you do can save you—
not when your hordes of fighters drop and die,
cut down by the hands of man-killing Hector![6]

I linger over Achilles, partly because this nonidealized form of dignity, dignity raging against the dishonor done to it, actually seems to me the more common form that it takes. This dignity needs to assert itself, at the expense of the lives of "hordes" of others—which suggests that this particular virtue might not be easily translatable from its individual form into a collective form, into an egalitarian model for everyone. What Achilles' rage points to is indeed a tragic world, in which slights and insults are likely to come our way, and to be met with a commensurate fury of response. Dignity, in this nonidealized world, stands as a kind of double-faced armed response, a defensive shield that, if necessary, can also go on the attack. And some kind of offensive action does seem to be in the script, since it is unlikely that this high self-esteem would not experience the world as an affront at some point, and would not feel justified to lash out at this perceived injury.

It is this nonidealized world that actually seems to me to be the foundation of law, because law too acts on the premise that injurability is a normative condition for human beings, a condition correlated with a claim for redress. Waldron sees dignity as the legal ground as well as the legal content for the exercise of rights. I think the connection between these two is strongest in the context of systemic vengeance—in the context, that is, of predictable grievance and predictable retaliation, an offending act being responded to in kind. But if that is indeed the case, if the foundation of jurisprudence is not a right that is respected but a right that is violated, then law would also seem to belong to the genre of tragedy, as much as dignity does, moving in exactly the same elevated and darkening universe that Homer and Aristotle have outlined for us.

And the convergence of law, dignity, and tragedy comes not only from the fact that all three inhabit a world in which human beings nurse grievances, but also because all three allow for an escalation of those grievances, since the high platform on which dishonor is imagined to have been suffered also means that the response will be on that platform as well. This seems to me to be one of the greatest dangers in a jurisprudence based on dignity, a concept conferring high privilege on everyone, but perhaps also involving a maintenance cost correspondingly high.

In conclusion, I would like to ask Waldron whether he could imagine a jurisprudence not quite operating at that level, something like a *low* jurisprudence, one that relaxes rather than tightens the demand for dignity. And, to frame this discussion, I'd like to invoke Aristotle once again and his remarks about one genre in particular that he specifically identifies as low, namely, comedy. *This* genre, he says, concerns itself with "persons who are inferior; not, however, going all the way to villainy," but rather giving itself the freedom to deal with "the ugly, of which the ludicrous is one part. The ludicrous, that is, is a failing, or a piece of ugliness which causes no pain or destruction."[7]

If tragedy is defined by the noble bearing of the protagonists, comedy is defined by those who are far below that ideal, those who look and act like fools and buffoons, but who also bring no catastrophes into the world. Waldron speaks of dignity as "moral orthopedics," standing tall in the world. I would like to end with a contrasting image, an image of two people down on all fours, in a poem that calls itself the *Commedia*.

The two people in question are Dante and Virgil. They are in hell, but since this is Canto 34 of the *Inferno*, they are just about to get out. And this is how they do it, by crawling on their hands and knees, scrambling up the body of Satan:

> He grabbed on to the shaggy sides of Satan;
> then downward, tuft by tuft, he made his way
> between the tangled hair and crust,

> When we had reached the point exactly where
> the thigh begins, right at the haunch's curve,
> my guide, with strain and force of every muscle,
>
> turned his head toward the shaggy shanks of Dis
> and grabbed the hair as if about to climb—
> I thought that we were heading back to Hell.
>
> "Hold tight, there is no other way," he said,
> panting, exhausted, "only by these stairs
> can we leave behind the evil we have seen."[8]

According to this interesting topography, the way out of hell is initially by going down. And *down* in several senses: going down the shanks of Satan, getting down on all fours, and allowing oneself to look downright ridiculous in the process. Perhaps because of his Christian heritage, dignity is not a prime consideration for Dante. It is the freedom not to look dignified that enables the poets to get out of the place where they have no wish to linger. Perhaps with a nod to Aristotle, Dante is indeed writing a comedy, a genre about people we can almost look down on, certainly people we can laugh at, but who do us no harm, and who will avoid harming themselves as far as possible. A nonidealized world, it seems, does not always have to lead to a tragic outcome, with dignity coming to a glorious but disastrous end. Dante's version is, of course, only poetry, not law. But I'd like to ask Waldron if he could imagine a jurisprudence in that spirit. If a jurisprudence of dignity is a tragic jurisprudence, what would a comic jurisprudence look like?

## Notes

1. Herman Melville, *Moby-Dick* (1851; New York: Signet, 1962), p. 123.
2. Ibid., pp. 123–24.
3. Aristotle, *Poetics,* trans. Gerald Else (Ann Arbor: University of Michigan Press, 1967), pp. 21, 24.

4. Homer, *The Iliad*, trans. Robert Fagles (New York: Penguin, 1990), p. 83.

5. Ibid.

6. Ibid., p. 85.

7. Aristotle, *Poetics*, p. 23.

8. Dante, *The Divine Comedy*, vol. 1, *Inferno*, trans. Mark Musa (New York: Penguin, 1984), pp. 381–82.

# Reply to Commentators

# Reply

JEREMY WALDRON

I am most grateful to my three commentators—Wai Chee Dimock, Don Herzog, and Michael Rosen—for these criticisms and suggestions. It is a matter of great good fortune for me that each of them understands and has some broad sympathy for the conception of human dignity that I am advancing and that each of them has offered numerous suggestions as to how that conception might be enriched as well as warnings about the pitfalls that I am prone to fall into as I develop it.

Between them, my commentators have focused on several specific claims that I tried to advance in the lectures.

1. One claim was about the proper habitat of "dignity" as a concept: I claimed that dignity is more at home in the law (including the philosophical and normative part of jurisprudence) than in morality considered apart from the law.

2. Another claim concerned the normative shape that dignity assumes: many philosophers think of it as a value; some treat it as the name of a principle; I think of it as a status. (Connected with this are some issues raised by Michael Rosen about dignity's relation to other concepts such as autonomy and respect, and some issues raised by Wai Chee Dimock about the relationship between dignity and the way in which people bear themselves or present themselves in moral, social, or life interactions.)

3. A third claim is about the character of the egalitarianism implicit in the modern concept of human dignity. Some think that human dignity must be sharply separated from the ideas

of social differentiation and hierarchy associated with the old Roman notion of *dignitas* and indeed from older uses of "dignity" in English. But I think the two are connected in a dynamic way: the modern concept of human dignity involves a sort of leveling up of everyone to something like the highest status that is consecrated in the older hierarchical conception. Don Herzog has some critical things to say about the way I develop this idea, and I take his criticism very seriously.

If my commentators will bear with me, I am going to develop some brief observations in reply to their criticisms theme-by-theme rather than commentator-by-commentator. This is because there are some very important overlaps between the suggestions that my commentators have been good enough to offer, and there are also important ways in which the comments of each of them cast some light upon the comments of the others. I want, if I may, to take advantage of this illumination.

## 1. Dignity's Habitat

I said in the lectures that we should take as our starting point the use that is made of dignity in law (particularly in international human rights law) rather than the sense that moral philosophers have been able to make of the term. Michael Rosen asks, quite properly, why we should not move back and forth between the legal context and the moral analysis. Of course he is right; by suggesting a particular starting point, I did not want to preclude this and I think the analysis in the lectures bears out my use of the back-and-forth approach.

Still, I want to insist that it is wise not to begin over in moral philosophy, particularly modern moral philosophy. Analysis in that environment is often destructive or, at best, reductive. Many of the moral philosophers I talk to about dignity begin by being quite skeptical about whether there is work for the concept to do that isn't already being done by other concepts (for example, value, autonomy, or respect). Their impulse seems to be that we should get by with as few normative concepts as possible—as though concepts were expensive. The flattening or impoverishment of our evaluative language is a virtue, not a drawback, for them. Not only that, but they approach "dignity" as though it were an obscure piece of metaphysical or theological jargon that, if allowed into respectable discourse, would contaminate and undermine the rigor of moral analysis. Eventually, no doubt, we have to consider such worries. But I prefer at least to begin by looking at the work that is actually being done by dignity in the legal environment, particularly as our sense of that work grows and develops rather than starting from the question, posed abstractly, of whether we "need" such a concept at all.

I said that my concern is primarily about the reaction of *modern* moral philosophers. Rosen is surely right that no discussion of dignity's role in the law is complete without considering the philosophical heritage—the Kantian heritage, for example (though he emphasizes other philosophical traditions as well)—that is associated with the present prominence of the concept in modern jurisprudence. For example, the role that dignity plays in the opening sections of the German Basic Law is undoubtedly affected by the Kantian conception of *Würde* in the *Groundwork*, for example, and the German Constitutional Court's decision-making has made very considerable use of this philosophical background.[1] (In fact, I am most grateful for the historical dimension of Rosen's comments.)

Wai Chee Dimock raises a different point about habitat—or, as she calls it, dignity's "proper home." She understands that, in my insistence on dignity's presence in the law, I have in mind not just the explicit references to dignity that one finds in human rights conventions, but also law's modus operandi—the fact that the characteristic modes of law's application and legal compliance are deeply dignitarian in their character. I greatly appreciate what she says about this. The point is one that I took initially from Lon Fuller and it has become increasingly important in my jurisprudential work since the Tanner Lectures were delivered.[2]

However, Dimock thinks that there is a danger of losing sight of other habitats in which dignity's claims are tested and explored. She has in mind particularly the domain of literature. And certainly the work she has done to tease out the theme of "democratic dignity" from Melville's *Moby Dick*—the "uncanny parallel" she discovers—was a revelation to me. (I shall say a little more, under subhead 3, "Equal Dignity," concerning her account of the tragically "high-maintenance" demands that dignity places on the *Pequod* and those who sail in her.) I am most grateful for this.

I wonder though whether regarding literature as a domain from which great insights about dignity can be drawn is on a par with regarding law as a primary habitat for dignity. As an alternative, literature seems to operate in a different sort of way. So, for example, one can imagine giving an account of (1) the ways in which legal systems (or social or moral systems) implicate and promote dignity and (2) the ways in which novelists or playwrights write about what legal systems (or social systems) do to implicate and promote dignity. In (2), we reflect—partly imaginatively—upon (1), which is quite a different things from seeing (1) and (2) as alternatives. The real rivalry is between legal systems and social or moral systems as domains for dignity's self-revelation, not between either system of that sort and a literary representation of it.

On this basis, then, perhaps what we should say is that the striking account that Dimock draws from *Moby Dick* counts as a reflection upon some of the informal ways in which dignity operates as a notion in social life. There is nothing specifically legal—though there may be something political—in Melville's chapter "Knights and Squires." So the alternative that is presented in the passages quoted by Dimock is best understood as a challenge to my position—to which Michael Rosen also takes exception—that "dignity does not crop up much in ordinary moral conversation." Even if that claim were true—and I think I am properly chastened by Rosen's demonstration that it is not—Dimock's example shows that a powerful sense of human dignity might nevertheless pervade ordinary social interactions (if the events on the deck of the *Pequod* can be called "ordinary") in ways that have little to do with legal proceedings.

I do think that contrasting the work of literary imagination and the drudgery of moral analysis is also fruitful. Reading Melville's account of democratic dignity ("that abounding dignity which has no robed investiture") I am convinced more than ever that the mean, cramped imperative of philosophical reductionism is not the tool we need to make sense of the work that this concept has to do in human affairs. Dignity is a concept that enriches our vocabulary: many of those riches arise in the first instance from law and from other formal aspects of our social organization. But I am happy to accept the insistence of all three of my commentators that we must also be willing to trace the extent of its influence in more informal domains.

## 2. Dignity's Shape

Michael Rosen thinks I have made a serious mistake by dissociating myself from those aspects of our philosophical and ecclesiastical heritage that present dignity as a value. Let me see if I can convince him that my approach—which treats dignity as a certain sort of status—is the sounder approach.

It is true that in Immanuel Kant's *Groundwork* and in the content of some of the relevant papal encyclicals, dignity is spoken of as a certain kind of value—a nonfungible value, in Kant's conception and a precious intrinsic value in the Catholic conception. Rosen also quotes a comment by Thomas Aquinas to the effect that the word "dignity" signifies something's goodness. My inclination—a little perverse perhaps—is not to take these formulations entirely at face value, if they indicate on their face a preference for a value conception rather than a status conception of dignity. The Aquinas formulation is the easiest to deal with: I know of no consistent or respectable use of "dignity" that treats it as a synonym for "goodness"—understood as a praiseworthy quality of conduct or the possession of virtue. Instead Aquinas's phraseology is immediately oriented to the standing and considerability that a being has on account of its creation or on its sharing (say) the image of God. And much the same happens in Kant and in modern Catholic thought. Were Kant to associate dignity purely with the nonfungible character of certain values—that which is "raised above all price and therefore admits of no equivalent"—we would be well advised to translate his term *Würde* with our term "worth" rather than "dignity." But Kant goes on elsewhere in his writings to associate *Würde* with a basis on which people might legitimately elicit respect from others and demand room, as it were, for their presence and their agency.[3] In this sense, dignity ceases to be a purely value-concept and takes on the character much more of a concept of normative status or considerability.

The contrast between the two can perhaps be illuminated by an analogy with citizenship. (Actually it is only partially an analogy: Kant explores the idea of the dignity proper to citizenship in his political philosophy.)[4] Citizenship is very important as indicating a status that individuals have, which dictates some of the fundamental ways in which they are to be treated and in which their presence and their actions are to be accommodated in the operation of a state or civil society. Someone might try to analyze citizenship in terms of the location of a certain value in each person; but it would be an awkward and unilluminating analysis. A citizen is not just a valuable asset of the state, nor is a citizen simply something of value in its own right, apart from its usefulness to the state. If we are talking of value at all here, we are talking of the value of something that is aware of its own value (and of whose value this awareness is one of the most important features) and that behaves accordingly—which is not, as it happens, the way we ordinarily think about values or the way we are prepared to think about values by something narrow called value theory. An analysis in terms of value or goodness, or a reduction of citizenship to these categories, would distort our understanding and fail to give an account of much that was important in that concept. I think that in trying to understand the concept of citizenship we would quickly find that a value analysis was inadequate.

Alternatively, we might try to pursue the matter in terms of a certain clustering of rights and duties: a citizen is one who has *these* rights and *these* duties (defined more or less by a list). This is one account I toy with in the lectures so far as status terms in general are concerned. But a status term is never just reducible to a list of rights and duties; it also conveys the *point* of clustering those particular rights and duties together in a certain way. And once again that point is not just a value or a telos; it is a matter of fleshing out and responding to a certain sort of standing or considerability that an entity or agent is supposed to have among us, in virtue of which things may be demanded of us and also of it. This is true of citizenship and I think it is also true of human dignity.

The idea of status is an underexplored normative category, both in law and in morality. It used to be spoken of in law much more than it is now, and in these lectures I took the opportunity to try to revive this exploration. More work is evidently needed (more will be forthcoming), and what there is here is necessarily a work in progress. I think that is true also of the analysis of dignity generally, by others as well as by me. Rosen is right that some of this analysis uses initially the language of value, as Kant did; but as we saw, it is quickly found necessary to tilt the analysis towards something like status, even if that tilt is not marked with the explicit use of the term.

Don Herzog has offered some very helpful comments about the distinction between status and role, which I am happy to appropriate. I suspect though that in some cases the two hook up more closely than he indicates, and I think this connection was exemplified in earlier hierarchical uses of "dignity" or the Roman *dignitas*. Caesar's being a great general—this was not just a role that he could "ordinarily shift in and out of." As a role or office, it had a sort of totalizing aspect that followed him "relentlessly" everywhere and took on many of the characteristics of status, as Herzog understands it. Maybe in the modern world, citizenship is also a role like this: a role that is also a status. Be that as it may, Herzog's underlying point is a most helpful one. There is something almost ontological about the way in which a status defines who a person is—this is particularly true of what I call in the lectures sortal status—and I think modern ideas of human dignity tap into that ontological aspect.

Herzog notes also that the status aspect of dignity is connected with modern doctrines of dignity's inalienability. One cannot forfeit human dignity "even by grotesque immorality." (I am reminded of Justice Emeritus Aharon Barak's stricture about terrorists in the Israeli targeted killing case: "Needless to say, unlawful combatants are not beyond the law....God created them as well in his image; their human dignity as well is to be honored; they as well enjoy and are entitled to protection...by customary international law.")[5]

Equally, however, one cannot give up the demands associated with dignity. Indeed one has a responsibility to maintain one's dignity—to be, as it were, a faithful steward of human dignity in one's person—and many of the rights associated with dignity are tinged with this responsibility.[6] There are aspects here that distinguish dignity from autonomy, with which it is often confused and to which, many have argued, all that is useful in dignity can be reduced.[7] But our modern understanding of autonomy sees it almost entirely as a matter of right untinged by any sense of responsibility. Once upon a time, autonomy carried with it a sense of responsibility; but now it is just a matter of choice and freedom. It operates as an emancipating concept in a straightforward way in which dignity does not. Dignity carries with it an obligation to maintain the elevated status to which one is called as a human being. So, for example, in the notorious French "dwarf-tossing" case—a municipality banned an activity that involved large men tossing little people along padded hallways or corridors, to see who could throw their dwarf the farthest[8]—an analysis in terms of autonomy would be quite different from an analysis in terms of dignity. I don't mean that the practice can be condemned uncontroversially on dignitarian grounds when autonomy requirements are satisfied (e.g., consent on the part of the dwarfs, with large payments being made to them to secure that consent), but on a dignitarian ground there is room for open debate about how the practice of dwarf-tossing implicates dignity, whereas on autonomy grounds such controversies are much harder to raise.[9]

Rosen is right, I think, to note, then, that there is tension at the heart of modern notions of human dignity as between the emphasis that is given to choice ("Dignity…requires individuals to be allowed the power of choice over matters that they consider to be of the highest importance to themselves") and the emphasis that is given to responsibility. I disagree however with his view that the antivoluntarist strain in this tension is represented solely by the Catholic conception of dignity as a value attaching to the human person. In fact the antivoluntarist strain is much better represented in status terms than in value terms. On the conception of dignity as a kind of value, one has to get into all sorts of contortions about the responsibility that a value owes to itself qua value. The implication from status to responsibility is much more straightforward. We find it in the traditional hierarchical notion of dignity—it is part of the dignity of a bishop or a judge, for example, that he limit his own choices in various ways. And it is not hard to bring out similar strains of responsibility with regard to human dignity as such. (At the risk of repetition, let me emphasize that this matter is not settled: those who talk of human dignity disagree about the extent of the responsibilities that it imposes upon its bearers.[10] But the question is necessarily raised by our notion of dignity, in a way that it isn't raised by our notions of autonomy or value, and there is space in and around the status conception of dignity for this debate to take place and for various intelligible positions to be staked out.)

Apart from the limits that responsibility might impose upon choice, there is also the question of the relation between dignity and self-regarding virtue. It is noteworthy that Kant located much of his discussion of dignity in the part of *The Metaphysics of Morals* devoted to personal ethics.[11] It is there that one finds his version of what I have called "moral orthopedics"—what Wai-Chee Dimock calls "nobility of demeanor" as a normative doctrine associated with dignity. I don't think I meant to imply in the lectures that this could be all that there was to dignity—as though such an account might rival and thus exist in tension with other aspects of the account that I gave. I don't think we should say that these virtues of standing up straight, and not presenting oneself in an abject or degraded matter, go to the heart of any plausible conception of dignity. I certainly did not mean to imply—as I think Dimock says—that "for there to be dignity, all it takes is for one person to feel this self-esteem." What I meant to say was that human dignity, like the older dignity of nobility, resonates with requirements of this kind: I don't think dignity could do the work that it demands of others unless it had some such resonance. And I do think this element of noble bearing is normatively important also for the way one is treated by others; one must not be treated by others in ways that make a degraded bearing or a degraded self-presentation unavoidable.

What, finally, about respect? What is the normative relation between dignity and respect? The syntax is a little loose here, enabling Michael Rosen to ask what the difference is between respecting a person and respecting that person's dignity. We use both phrases: sometimes they are more or less synonymous, with the clearer formulation being that a person's dignity generates a duty to respect that person (in various ways); sometimes the second formulation connotes something slightly more specific, roughly what Rosen calls "respect-as-respectfulness," which has to do with avoiding the imposition of specifically dignitary harms like insulting and degrading treatment. I don't in any way want to minimize this latter aspect of respect, and I don't think Rosen does either, not even when he says that it concerns only "expressive or symbolic harms...in which the elevated status of human beings *fails to be acknowledged.*" But Rosen is right that respect for persons *simpliciter* takes in a wider range of duties, many of which are more important and more fundamental than respect-as-respectfulness. (With characteristic directness he insists: "[T]he worst of what the Nazi state did to the Jews was not the humiliation...; it was to murder them.")

The fact that respect for persons includes not murdering them (and much else besides) and the conceptual point that dignity requires respect for persons—these might lead one to conclude that dignity is the foundation of all rights and of almost all important duties that we owe to other people. In a sense it is, and that is conveyed by the invocations of dignity in the preambles to the great human rights conventions. But the foundations of our most important duties are complex and tangled. Dignity is not the whole story of what we most fundamentally owe to others; it is not the whole story of the wrongness of killing, for example, nor, as Rosen remarks, is it the whole story of the wrongness of torture. But it works in the foundations, complementing whatever else is working there, not least because, as Rosen says at the very end of his comment, failures in the apprehension of people's human dignity may make it much easier for others to engage in the most violent behavior towards them.

## 3. Equal Dignity

I am heartened by the fact that all three of my commentators find something helpful and stimulating in my lectures' most prominent thesis—that modern human dignity represents a sort of normative leveling-up to the treatment and respect that traditionally was due only to those occupying the topmost rungs in society's hierarchy of status.

In the lectures, and in some earlier work, I pursued this thesis by using a sort of thought experiment: I invited my readers to consider the privileges of high aristocratic rank, and to consider what things would be like if those privileges were accorded to everyone. Of course some of those privileges might be positional: a high noble might have the right to speak first in any debate about the kingdom's affairs, and that cannot be universalized. But with others, universalization is possible; for some it is interestingly transformative (like transforming a right to be consulted in the affairs of the kingdom into something like one vote among millions in a system of universal suffrage); for others, universalization may preserve the content and understanding of a right, but just alter the way in which political morality operates (I had in mind here as an example the aristocrat's right not to be struck.)[12]

A thought experiment of this kind has its risks. The institution and culture of aristocracy has all sorts of features, many of them associated specifically with the reservation of nobility's privileges to a few. So, for example, those haughty individuals who enjoyed these privileges might have associated with them a sort of mentality that was arrogant, condescending, abusive, lawless, irresponsible, willful, and violent. Don Herzog invites my audience to consider these aspects of noble status, too, and he seeks to cast doubt on my thought experiment by discrediting it with one of his own, in which we generalize and make pervasive within a democratic culture the mentality as well as the nonpositional privileges that interest me. As always, he makes his point well—forcefully and at length.

One might just abandon the thought experiment and talk more abstractly about the generalization of high-status treatment, without specifying any concrete institution or practice from which the character of high-status treatment was to be inferred. After all, the thought experiment was supposed to be illustrative, not definitional, and Herzog might be right in his conclusion that it is less illuminating than distracting.

But I am reluctant to abandon it altogether in the face of his criticism, partly because I think his criticism is helpful and revealing. I think Herzog is right to suggest that it may not be easy to separate noble mentality from noble privilege. And we may not want to: it is part of the human dignity idea that people aware of themselves as having this status will come to think of themselves in a distinctive way—and will put that thinking on display for others to see. (Sometimes this will seem comic, in the way that Dimock intimates, and sometimes—as Herzog suggests in his example of Robert Peel— the comedy will leave room for sneering condescension.) Moreover, the generalized noble privileges that arise out of human dignity may not be associated with the old arrogance of nobility, but there will be something like haughtiness—horizontal haughtiness, I would like to say—and formality and even ritual in the way dignified people bear themselves. We may not want human dignity to be associated with the kind of lashing-out at presumptuous members of the lower orders that characterized the old nobility; but we will expect it to be associated with a furious sense of one's rights and a willingness to stand up for them as part of what it means to stand up for what is best and most important in oneself. (In saying all this, I am conscious of Wai Chee Dimock's reading of *Moby Dick*, in which the exigencies of high-maintenance dignity can also generate tragic costs and dilemmas when that dignity is generalized in a particular setting. The emphasis that we put on generalized haughtiness might make it more difficult to develop principles of fallibility, reasonableness, give-and-take, and proper humility, in a dignitarian world. That remains a challenge.)

In other regards, too, there will have to be reconstruction. I associated the high privilege generalized as human dignity with a certain standing and responsibility before the law. Herzog reminds us that aristocratic privilege was associated as much with an abusive lack of legal accountability as with formal forensic responsibility

before one's peers. The nobles, endowed as they were with oppositional privilege, might have been strangers to legal accountability;
and so establishing a world of human dignity will have to put an
end to that estrangement. So: simple universalization is not sufficient to characterize what has to go into this new world of leveled-
up dignity.

All that I accept. There is a more dangerous edge (for my argument), however, in a suggestion that Herzog makes that some of
the high-status legal treatment that I want to generalize is just an
artifact of aristocratic legal irresponsibility: "I enjoy special privileges and need not answer to the likes of you for how I use them."
I mentioned the Countess of Rutland, whose body could not be
seized for debt; and now, I say, nobody's body can be seized for debt.
Is this a generalization of a more respectful mode of legal accountability, or is it a generalization of the complete lack of legal accountability that characterized the aristocratic mentality? Well, there
may be room for debate in some cases, but not in this one. I think
we have worked out respectful ways of responsibility for debt,
rather than ways of generalizing contempt for one's creditors. The
same may be said concerning the form and character of punishment. Previously there were modes of incarceration and execution
reserved for nobility, and different and much more painful and degrading modes of incarceration and execution that applied to commoners. Some countries have generalized the aristocratic modes, in
pursuance of what they regard as human dignity; others have not,
or done so only partially. But it would be wrong to suggest that
those that have, have failed to keep faith with legal accountability.
They don't allow people to evade legal coercion and punishment
when that is appropriate; they just coerce and punish in what is
ultimately a more respectful way. If Herzog's point is that we need
to bring discernment to this thought experiment, then I am sure he
is right. But I don't believe this undermines the usefulness of this
way of thinking.

I have not done justice to everything in these most helpful comments. But I hope to have shown my commentators that I take what they have said very seriously and that I am happy and grateful to use it in correcting and enriching my account.

## Notes

1. We saw this for example in what has become known as the German airliner decision, which I referred to in section 6 of my first lecture. Cf. Lecture 1, footnote 47.

2. See Fuller, *The Morality of Law*, p. 162. See also Jeremy Waldron, "How Law Protects Dignity: The 2010 Sir David Williams Lecture," *Cambridge Law Review* 71 (2012): 200.

3. Kant, *The Metaphysics of Morals*, p. 557 (6:434–35): "[A] human being regarded as a person…possesses a dignity (an absolute inner worth) by which he exacts respect for himself from all other beings in the world."

4. Ibid., p. 471 (6:330): "Certainly no human being in a state can be without dignity, since he has at least the dignity of a citizen."

5. *The Public Committee against Torture in Israel and Palestinian Society for the Protection of Human Rights and the Environment v. The Government of Israel and Others* (HCJ 769/02) December 11 2005, § 25. See also the discussion in Waldron, "The Image of God," at p. 225.

6. I have developed this aspect further in the Shoen Lecture I gave at Arizona State University Law School in October 2010, published as "Dignity, Rights and Responsibilities," *Arizona State University Law Journal* 43 (2012): 1107.

7. Michael Rosen refers to one such reductive attempt in Ruth Macklin's essay "Dignity Is a Useless Concept," in the *British Medical Journal*.

8. Conseil d'État, October 27, 1995, Rec. Lebon 372, available at http://www.conseil-etat.fr/fr/presentation-des-grands-arrets/27-octobre-1995-commune-de-morsang-sur-orge.htm.

9. It might be controversial in relation to the liberal perfectionism of Joseph Raz's conception of autonomy in *The Morality of Freedom* (Oxford: Clarendon Press, 1986). But Raz's conception of autonomy is a

peculiar one, centered in the idea that autonomous choice has no value when it is not itself oriented to value.

10. See, e.g., Stephanie Hennette-Vauchez, "A Human *Dignitas*? Remnants of the Ancient Legal Concept in Contemporary Dignity Jurisprudence," *International Journal of Constitutional Law* 9 (2011): 32; and Christopher McCrudden, "Human Dignity and Judicial Interpretation of Human Rights," *European Journal of International Law* 19 (2008): 655.

11. Kant, *The Metaphysics of Morals*, pp. 558–59 (6:436).

12. See also Waldron, "Dignity and Rank," p. 201.

# Index

Lightning Source UK Ltd.
Milton Keynes UK
UKOW01f2307191017
311297UK00001B/12/P